Please Scan This QR Code Before You Begin Reading This Book

Video Instructions From Dr. Joses Ngugi

Unlock Your Hidden Income

A Step-by-Step Guide for Young Adults to Monetize Their Skills and Achieve Financial Freedom

Dr. Joses Ngugi

Tri Star Publishing

PUBLISHED BY: Tri Star Publishing

www.TriStarPublishing.info

DISCLAIMER AND/OR LEGAL NOTICES: While all attempts have been made to verify information provided in this book and its ancillary materials, neither the author or publisher assumes any responsibility for errors, inaccuracies or omissions and is not responsible for any financial loss by customer in any manner. Any slights of people or organizations are unintentional. If advice concerning legal, financial, accounting or related matters is needed, the services of a qualified professional should be sought. This book and its associated ancillary materials, including verbal and written training, is not intended for use as a source of legal, financial or accounting advice. You should be aware of the various laws governing business transactions or other business practices in your particular geographical location.

EARNINGS & INCOME DISCLAIMER: With respect to the reliability, accuracy, timeliness, usefulness, adequacy, completeness, and/ or suitability of the information provided in this book, Dr. Joses Ngugi, Cash In Class University LLC, its partners, associates, affiliates, consultants, and/or presenters make no warranties, guarantees, representations, or claims of any kind. Readers' results will vary depending on a number of factors. Any and all claims or representations as to income earnings are not to be considered as average earnings. Testimonials are not representative. This book and all products and services are for educational and informational purposes only. Use caution and see the advice of qualified professionals. Check with your accountant, attorney or professional advisor before acting on this or any information. You agree that Dr. Joses Ngugi and/or Cash In Class University LLC is not responsible for the success or failure of your personal, business, health or financial decisions relating to any information presented by Dr. Joses Ngugi, Cash In Class University LLC, or company products/services. Earnings potential is entirely dependent on the efforts, skills and application of the individual person. Any examples, stories, references, or case studies are for illustrative purposes only and should not be interpreted as testimonies and/or examples of what reader and/or consumers can generally expect from the information. No representation in any part of this information, materials and/or seminar training are guarantees or promises for actual performance. Any statements, strategies, concepts, techniques, exercises and ideas in the information, materials and/or seminar training offered are simply opinion or experience, and thus should not be misinterpreted as promises, typical results or guarantees (expressed or implied). The author and publisher (Dr. Joses Ngugi, Cash In Class University LLC or any representatives) shall in no way, under any circumstances, be held liable to any party (or third party) for any direct, indirect, punitive, special, incidental or other consequential damages arising directly or indirectly from any use of books, materials and or seminar trainings, which is provided "as is," and without warranties.

Dedication

To my amazing wife, Eliana Ngugi.

Your unwavering belief in me, even when I doubted myself, has been my greatest source of strength. Your endless inspiration and boundless support have carried me through the toughest times and fueled our journey to success. God knew exactly what He was doing when He planted me right next to you! This book, dedicated to helping young adults unlock their hidden income and achieve financial freedom, is a testament to your love, patience, and the countless sacrifices you've made to help me pursue my dreams. Thank you for being my rock and my biggest cheerleader.

This is for you.

Acknowledgements

This book has been a journey of transformation, fueled by the support, wisdom, and encouragement of many remarkable individuals.

First and foremost, I want to thank my incredible wife, Eliana Ngugi, and our wonderful children, Neriah and Nehvea. Your unwavering love, patience, and belief in me have been my greatest source of strength. Your sacrifices and understanding have made this dream a reality.

To my parents, Mom and Dad, calling you Joseph and Mary would feel very disrespectful in our culture. Thank you for instilling in me the values of hard work and perseverance. Your journey as immigrants to this country, your unwavering faith in God, and showing us how there is nothing we could not get through if we are aligned with God's will for our lives have been a big part of my guiding light. Your dedication to our family has been my beacon of hope.

To my siblings, Chris and Joy, I express my deepest gratitude for everything you have taught me without even realizing it. Watching you both go for your dreams and tap into the most authentic versions of yourselves has inspired me to relentlessly pursue what I have been called to do, without fear of what others might think or say, because we truly only get one shot at this life. Thank you both so much, and I pray that you continue to tap into everything that you are capable of and continue to inspire the world in more ways than anyone can imagine.

To Dr. Casey Coleman, my business partner and close friend, everything that we are living now doesn't happen without you. What I'm uncovering in this book truly came from our conversations, and what we've been able to build together has not only changed the lives of the people we've worked with, but has also transformed my life. For that, I thank you.

To all my mentors. I am deeply grateful to all of my mentors, but the one I truly want to highlight is my very first mentor, Greg Todd. You opened the way for me and my family, and there is a very special place in my heart for you and your family because of what you have shown us is possible, not only in business and life, but also in faith and family. I am eternally grateful for you. Everything that I am today goes back to what I learned from you. While I've had many coaches and mentors after you, you hold a very special place in my heart and my family's heart.

To my close friends and confidants, DJ Haskins, Gabi Pasos, Javi Carlin, Marissa Carlin, Andrea Rice, Kyle Rice, Paul Ochieng, and Danielle Ochieng, your unwavering support and encouragement have kept me going even in the toughest times. Thank you for your belief in me and your constant motivation.

I also want to thank Alayna Zenger, who has been a key piece of our Cash in Class University team. You have brought all of our coaching programs in our company to life, creating an experience for our clients that has far exceeded anything we have ever seen or done before. A lot of the transformations happening with our clients in their journeys as they build their moneymakers are because of the experience, detail, presence, and expertise you have brought to our team. Thank you so much for that.

Additionally, I want to thank the many other guests who have played a role in helping us build this movement over the years as we seek to help reshape how people look at their ability to build the lives of their dreams.

There are many other names I have not mentioned directly, but who have been pivotal in this journey and will continue to be pivotal in this journey and movement. Even if your name was not mentioned, please know that I am deeply grateful for your support and contributions.

A heartfelt thank you to all of our students and clients in our Build My Moneymaker Bootcamp, Impact To Income University, and New-Money Six-Figure Mastermind. Your stories, successes, and resilience have been a constant source of inspiration. Your journeys remind me daily of the impact and importance of this work.

Lastly, to my readers, thank you for embarking on this journey with me. Your curiosity, enthusiasm, and dedication to self-improvement inspire me every day. I hope this book serves as a beacon of hope and a guide towards financial freedom and personal empowerment.

Thank you all for being part of this incredible journey. This book would not have been possible without each and every one of you.

Thank you, Joses

Contents

Special <u>FREE</u> Bonus Gift for You!

To help you achieve more success, there are **FREE BONUS RESOURCES FOR YOU at:**

www.FreeGiftFromJoses.com

Working With Dr. Joses Ngugi and His Team

"As a student, I've secured over seven paying clients in just five months of starting this journey, thanks to Joses & Casey. Their guidance has been invaluable, and the skills I've learned have had a significant impact beyond the scope of medicine as a future healthcare provider."

– **Joel Mathew,** Impact To Income University Client

"Joses, In the last 50 days I have made $50,000! That's like $1,000 per day and I'm bad at math!"

– **Briana Drapp,** New Money 6 Figure Mastermind Client

"Before working with Joses & Casey, I was an emotional wreck and fed up. I decided never to feel that way again. This program has been the vehicle for living my dream. I'd tell anyone to jump in and not let fear rob them of an abundant, purpose-driven life. In just 95 days, I've already served more people than I can count."

– ***Ashley Baylor,*** Impact To Income University Client

"I started working with Joses and Casey last year to help healthcare professionals communicate with Spanish-speaking patients. Just months later, I made my first offer and earned $2,000 in a day, all before starting Physical Therapy School!"

– **Alejandro Fernandez,** Impact To Income University Client

"Following Casey and Joses' advice, I used my resources and offered an opportunity to my audience. One Instagram story post generated $1,000 in less than 48 hours, with an additional $1,100+ from the waitlist. If I had leveraged this sooner, I would have achieved these results much faster!"

– **Robyn Ringberg,** New Money 6 Figure Mastermind Client

"My "thing" that I am good at is scholarships, and to date, I've earned over $180,000 in academic scholarships. Working with Joses and Casey showed me how to turn my talent into a money maker. Now, I help other students master the scholarship game. I'm grateful for this journey, as it allows me to make money beyond school while doing what I'm passionate about."

– **Michaela Spencer,** Impact To Income University Client

"I 1,000% recommend working with Joses and Casey to any go-getter starting their journey. They transformed my mindset about my ability to impact others and generate income. I've met amazing people and made lifelong connections. Joses and Casey are incredible mentors. Absolutely recommend."

– **Nicole Mondragon,** Impact To Income University Client

"Joses and Casey helped me realize my dreams can become reality. They provided the resources, understanding, and confidence I needed to build my money maker. Now, the vision for my family and myself is tangible. I'm excited to share my talent, provide value, and earn an income. This has been an amazing experience that I wouldn't trade for anything."

– **Joseph Morphonios,** Impact To Income University Client

"Before working with Joses and Casey, I struggled with direction in my business. Their guidance gave me confidence, focus, and the push I needed to grow a business I love. The community and resources kept me committed and fearless. Inspired by their success stories, I aimed to work part-time by graduation. This experience proved that quitting is the only way to fail."

– **Alexa Rivera,** Impact To Income University Client

"I was hesitant to join, having tried other coaches before. However, Joses and Casey's intentionality, clarity and energy blew me away. I am now surrounded by passionate, like-minded people. This experience has changed my beliefs and mindset. I highly recommend Joses and Casey to anyone passionate about starting a money maker. Take the leap—it's worth it."

– **Germaine-Blaise Nkede,** Impact To Income University Client

The Ideal Speaker for Your Next Event?

Elevate your next event, online training, or gathering with the transformative insights of
Dr. Joses Ngugi.

Whether you're hosting an event or part of a group, Dr. Ngugi's engaging style will inspire your audience to uncover their unique gifts and turn them into impactful, income-generating opportunities.

Ready to bring transformative change to your next event?

To Contact or Book Dr. Joses Ngugi to Speak:

Visit josespeaks.com to schedule a speaking engagement

Foreword - Greg Todd

Business Coach, Entrepreneur CEO of Smart Success Health Care

When I first met Joses Ngugi, he had just become a client in my flagship program at the time, Smart Success PT, during his last year of physical therapy school. I had already been working with his now business partner, Casey Coleman, for a few months. Casey introduced Joses to my platform and program. From the beginning, Joses' drive and determination were clear—he didn't just talk about wanting a better life; he showed it through his actions.

It was obvious that Joses was hungry to figure things out. At the time, he and Casey were hosting a free program on their campus, not realizing it could be turned into a legitimate business. This venture became their first business, and it was just the beginning.

Despite the timing not being convenient—Joses was in his last clinical rotation in San Antonio, Texas, struggling financially as a student—he and Casey made it to my very first live event in Tampa. Joses often tells me that although he was only able to stay for 24 hours, that event completely changed the trajectory of his life and his family's life. That kind of commitment is rare, and it's clear to see the impact it has had.

Our relationship evolved from mentor and mentees to good friends. Joses eventually moved to Tampa, which has allowed us to work together more closely and deepen our bond. There's a lot you learn about someone when you see them face-to-face and interact with them regularly. You see their character, drive, and authenticity in ways that aren't always visible online.

"Unlock Your Hidden Income" reflects the lessons Joses and Casey have learned, not only from my teachings but also from their own journey building their business. This book is packed with practical advice and strategies that can help anyone break free from financial constraints and realize their true potential. Joses shares his own experiences and provides actionable steps that can be applied immediately.

This book is written with authenticity and a genuine desire to help others succeed. The insights shared into leveraging your skills, using technology, and creating new income streams are invaluable.

Joses doesn't just offer theories—he provides real-world solutions based on his own journey. His approach is about more than just making money; it's about creating a life that aligns with your values and passions. He's lived these principles and seen the results firsthand.

As you dive into this book, I urge you to fully engage with its content. This book is more than just advice; it's a guide to help you uncover gifts and skills you already have that can impact the world and change the trajectory of your family's life.

Joses, I'm proud of the work you and Casey have done and the impact you're making. This book stands as a testament to your dedication and remarkable journey. I'm excited for everyone who reads it to experience the same transformation you've achieved.

Best,

- Greg Todd

Preface

As a child, I experienced a profound fear of being trapped. I vividly remember an incident when I was ten years old, stuck in an old elevator in Indiana with family friends. The panic, the helplessness, and the overwhelming sense of being out of control stayed with me long after the doors finally opened. This fear of entrapment, whether physical or financial, has been a recurring theme in my life.

Growing up, I watched my parents work tirelessly as immigrants striving to build a better life in the United States. Despite their relentless efforts, financial security seemed perpetually out of reach. Their struggles became mine, shaping my views on work, money, and success. I followed the prescribed path: get a good education, secure a stable job, and work hard. Yet, even after earning a doctorate in physical therapy, I found myself feeling just as trapped as I did in that elevator—burdened by debt and confined by a career that didn't offer the freedom I desired.

This book is the result of my journey to break free from those constraints. It's a journey that took me from traditional employment to discovering entrepreneurial avenues, leveraging online platforms, and ultimately finding ways to generate sustainable and lucrative income. Along the way, I realized that hard work alone isn't enough; it's about working smart, leveraging your unique strengths, and embracing new opportunities.

I wrote this book for everyone who feels stuck in their current financial situation. Whether you're a student drowning in debt, a new grad struggling to make ends meet, or simply someone longing for more freedom and security, this book is for you. My goal is to provide you with the insights, strategies, and motivation you need to transform your financial reality and achieve true freedom.

In these pages, you'll find a blend of personal stories, practical advice, and actionable steps designed to help you take control of your financial future. I'll share the lessons I've learned, the mistakes I've made, and the successes I've achieved. Together, we'll explore how to challenge conventional wisdom about money, discover your unique moneymaker, and create a life that aligns with your dreams and values.

To my family, friends, and mentors—thank you for your unwavering support and belief in my vision. To my business partner, Dr. Casey Coleman—your vision and partnership have been instrumental in this journey. Your unwavering support and shared dreams have transformed my life and this book. To my readers—thank you for taking this journey with me. I hope this book inspires you, empowers you, and equips you to break free from financial constraints and live the life you've always dreamed of.

Welcome to the start of your new financial freedom.

Joses

A MESSAGE TO YOU

Break Free From The 'Broke' Cycle

A Message to You!

Break Free From The 'Broke' Cycle

Have you ever wondered what it would be like to not worry about money, loans, or bills anymore? Imagine making real money without needing another degree. What would it feel like to bless and take care of your family once you've figured it out?

As you begin this book, you might already be assuming that this might be too hard or that it may not be possible for you. You might even initially resist the ideas you're about to uncover. But remember this quote by Jim Kwik:

"If you fight for your limits, you get to keep them."

If you fight for the belief that it's impossible for you, that this won't work, that you don't already have the gifts and talents to make real money now while impacting hundreds, thousands, or more – or that you don't have the time or resources – then congratulations, you get to keep those limits. Just remember, those limits are simply a decision away from being shattered.

But if you are ready to stop fighting for your limits, I would love to share with you some strategies, principles, and tools that can help you start making more money sooner than you think. Whether you're a student, a new grad, or just someone trying to escape the trap of debt and financial worry, in the next few chapters, you'll start unlocking the secrets to having more time, more money, and more freedom. Starting now!

If this doesn't sound like what you want, this book may not be for you. But if you're already saying, **"Yes, show me how,"** keep reading.

Breaking Money Myths

This book is here to shatter the myths that have kept so many of us stuck in a relentless cycle of debt and financial frustration. You know the ones: **"Making more money is hard," "Only a select few can achieve financial success," "Earning too much is selfish or greedy," "More college or graduate schooling is the only path to financial security.** " Sound familiar? What if I told you these beliefs are nothing more than myths we've been fed since childhood?

This book is about unleashing your mind and tapping into the strengths and gifts you already possess. Imagine turning those gifts into solutions for real problems that people are facing right now, especially online. This isn't just about making money; it's about achieving financial freedom and gaining the time and independence you crave.

We're going to challenge the status quo and deliver practical solutions. I'll guide you through a powerful 5-step framework that has transformed the lives of countless clients, students, and professionals. Whether you're buried in student debt, feeling trapped in a dead-end career, or yearning for a more independent and fulfilling way to work, this book is your blueprint for change.

Why Now?

Let's dive into the problem we're tackling head-on. The cost of education is skyrocketing, but post-graduation paychecks just aren't keeping pace. Students are buried under crushing debt, sometimes over six figures, before they even hit their mid-twenties. Many of us wrestle with the fear that we're not good enough or skilled enough to help people and earn more now, whether we're students, new grads, or simply trying to navigate our lives.

Consider this: the average student debt stands at about $113,000. In the U.S., total student debt has ballooned to $1.77 trillion. For those in physical therapy, the average debt for a Doctor of Physical Therapy program is around $150,000, with some facing up to $230,000. Yet, the average income for new graduates in this field is only $75,000 to $80,000 a year before taxes. After taxes, you're left with about $58,000 annually, which breaks down to $4,833 a month. When you factor in rent, food, bills, emergencies, savings, retirement, kids, and those loan payments, you're likely living paycheck to paycheck or worse, relying heavily on credit cards even as a licensed professional.

Is this what you signed up for? Did you envision a life of constant debt juggling and financial struggle because you didn't know how to generate more income?

We've been taught that the only way to make more is to go to more school, but that's just not true anymore. We're living in a world where people are drowning in six-figure debt for careers that cap at $70,000 to $80,000 a year. The cost of living keeps climbing, and many feel hopelessly trapped.

But here's the good news: there has never been a better time to leverage the strengths and gifts you already have to make a real impact and turn that impact into serious money. One of the greatest cheat codes available today is AI. Artificial intelligence has leveled the playing field, allowing you to achieve in days or weeks what used to take years. Thanks to technology and the paths blazed by those who've gone before you, it's almost impossible to fail. The only thing standing between you and your financial freedom is the decision to start now.

My Promise

Here's my promise to you: I'm all in. I'm here to give you everything I've got. With your permission, I'm going to keep it real, cut out the fluff, and show you how things really work. Some of what you uncover might make you uncomfortable at first. But if you let me take you on this journey and keep it 100% real with you, it will drastically change your life.

What's Ahead

In a moment, you're about to unlock some game-changing secrets. Imagine graduating debt-free and being able to use your money for your life instead of drowning in loans. Picture making money right now, even if you feel like you have nothing people would pay for. You'll uncover blueprints that can help you earn between $2,000 and $30,000+ per month—whether you're still in school, a new grad, or just starting out in life. Imagine being able to gain more time to do what you love and spending it with the people who matter most. And most importantly, you'll find out how to unlock the freedom to choose your path and design your life exactly the way you want it.

Get ready, because what you're about to discover will make it hard to put this book down.

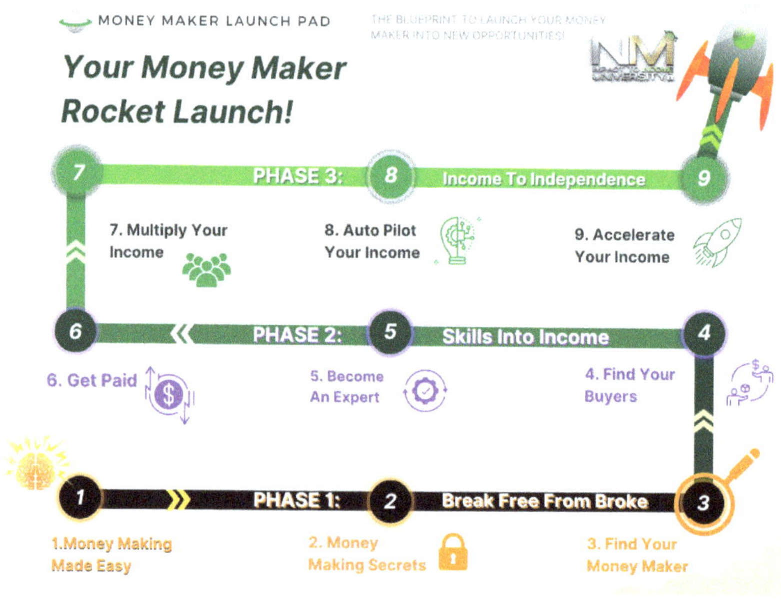

Your Roadmap

This book is your guide to breaking free from old constraints and stepping into a new reality with practical, actionable steps. Here's what you can expect to uncover in each chapter:

1. **No One Is Coming to Save You**
   - Learn why taking personal responsibility is crucial and how to overcome the obstacles that hold you back.
2. **The Hard Work Myth**
   - Discover why working smarter, not harder, is the key to achieving more with less effort.
3. **Unshackling Your Money Beliefs**
   - Challenge and transform the limiting beliefs about money that have been ingrained since childhood.
4. **Unlocking Your Unique Moneymaker**
   - Identify your unique skills and passions, and learn how to turn them into a profitable venture.
5. **Profit from Your Passion**
   - Learn to transition from offering free value to securing paying clients, effectively monetizing your expertise.
6. **Elevate to Premium**
   - Discover the strategies to elevate your offerings and command higher prices by providing exceptional value.
7. **Leverage for Exponential Growth**
   - Utilize time, technology, and people to grow your impact and income exponentially.

8. **Building Your Legacy**
    - Focus on creating a legacy that impacts your family, community, and the world, leaving an enduring mark that transcends wealth.

Each step is designed to build on the last, giving you a clear, actionable path. By the end of this book, you'll not only know what to do but have the confidence to go out and do it.

Is This You?

This book is for anyone who's had enough of feeling trapped by financial stress and debt. It's for:

- Students overwhelmed by debt, searching for a way out.
- New grads struggling to find their footing and make ends meet.
- Young adults eager for financial freedom and tired of the traditional 9-to-5 grind.
- Anyone who's disillusioned with the current ways of making a living and is hungry for practical, achievable alternatives.

If you're ready to break free from financial constraints, tap into your unique strengths and gifts, and create a life of abundance and freedom, then this book is for you.

Why Me?

So why should you listen to me? Why this book? Why now? Because I've been where you are, feeling the weight of uncertainty and the desire for something more. I am a husband of five years to my beautiful wife, Eliana, and a father to our two wonderful children, Neriah and Nehvea. By training, I'm a Doctor of Physical Therapy, but my journey didn't stop there. I've had the privilege of growing into a multi-business owner, public speaker, consultant, and business/sales coach. Since 2017, my team and I have been dedicated to helping thousands of students unlock their potential.

I understand what it's like to search for your purpose as a student and young professional. The frameworks and guidance I'll share in this book are the very ones that helped me find my path and build a life beyond what I once thought possible. Today, as the co-founder and CEO of two businesses generating over seven figures, my goal is to help you discover and achieve your potential too.

My business partner, Casey Coleman, has been an invaluable part of this journey. Casey's own experiences and insights have greatly enriched our mission. Together, we've developed a system that truly transforms lives. Casey's dedication and strategic thinking have been key in creating the frameworks and strategies we're excited to share with you.

This book isn't just about reading and hoping for change. It's about taking action. No one is coming to save you; it's up to you to take control. If you're ready to commit to this journey, keep reading. If not, close this book and gift it to someone ready to learn and take massive action now.

Let's begin.

CHAPTER 1

No one Is Coming to Save You

Chapter 1

No one Is Coming to Save You

Discovering Self-Reliance and Overcoming Traps

Ever since I can remember, the fear of being trapped without control has haunted me. This fear shaped my life, starting from a quiet summer evening in Indiana when I was just 10. After a long day at a conference, my family and some friends and I piled into a creaky elevator, joking and laughing—until it suddenly stopped.

The lights flickered, and a heavy silence filled the space. We were trapped. Panic set in. My heart raced, my breathing grew heavy, and tears welled up. I called out for my mom, my voice shaking with fear. The adults tried to reassure us, but I could see the worry in their eyes. We pressed buttons, pounded on the doors, and shouted for help, but there was no response. Time seemed to stretch endlessly, each minute feeling like an eternity.

Feeling Trapped

That childhood incident wasn't just a scary memory—it sparked a recurring theme in my life: the fear of being trapped without escape. This fear followed me into adulthood, influencing every decision I made—from my career to my finances and relationships. The fear of being stuck, of having no way out, is paralyzing. It's not just physical confinement—it's about feeling powerless.

Self-Reflection:

- What are your biggest fears related to feeling trapped or powerless in your life?
- Write them down and reflect on how these fears have impacted your decisions and actions.

Fast forward to a few months ago, I found myself on a small, old Silver Airways plane, returning from a keynote engagement in Fort Lauderdale. Desperate to get back to my wife and kids in Tampa, I took the earliest flight. Unease crept in as I boarded the aged aircraft. The tight, cramped space added to my anxiety. Turbulence hit almost immediately, shaking the plane violently. For 90 minutes, I was gripped by fear, every jolt heightening my sense of helplessness. This experience reignited my childhood fears, reinforcing my determination to never feel that way financially.

This fear of being trapped isn't just about turbulent flights or stalled elevators. It's about feeling stuck in life, in situations where you feel like you have no control. I know this feeling all too well, not just from my experiences but from my family's journey as well.

Evaluate Your Time:

How do you currently spend your time?

____

____

Are there areas where you feel you are investing too much time with little return or satisfaction?

____

____

Starting Over

My family immigrated from Kenya when I was six, chasing the American dream. Before moving, my parents had successful careers. My mom worked for the government, and my dad was an accountant and auditor. But in America, they had to start from scratch. My parents were forced to start all over after having had successful careers in Kenya. They started out both working at a local grocery store during the day. My dad even took some shifts at a factory at night. On top of that, they both went back to school to get better-paying jobs.

Reflect on Your Journey:

- Can you relate to starting from scratch, despite having a successful past?
- How has this impacted your view on work, time, and success?

I started to notice that time was limited. Time with my parents as a child was limited because they had to start over. They needed to invest their time and energy into building up again from scratch. This created new stresses, and our freedom and flexibility as a family were also very limited.

Visualize Freedom:

- What would a life of financial freedom, time, and flexibility look like for you?
- Describe your ideal day, week, and month in detail.

I remember at a very young age, somewhere between six years and eight years old, making a decision. I decided that I wanted to create a different life for my future family. I wanted to create a life where we would have more time, specifically at home with my future wife and kids, as well as less financial worries. Don't misunderstand me, I am extremely grateful for the sacrifices my parents made. They did what they had to do with the resources they had. But I came to realize that I didn't want to follow the same script. I wanted to do something different. I wanted to create a life where we had more time, more money, and more freedom/flexibility.

Whichever career I would choose needed to give me all three: time, money, and freedom.

I thought physical therapy was the answer. A physician once told me, "Joses, if I could do things over, I'd be a physical therapist. They have more freedom and less debt." That was all I needed to go all in on PT. I was a focused student, determined to succeed.

Debt Trap

But during my second year in PT school, my dream started to unravel. A conversation with a friend about finances revealed a harsh truth: even with an $80K salary, after taxes, rent, and other expenses, $80,000 didn't go as far as we thought. We were going to be doctors, but we'd still be struggling financially. It didn't add up. This realization was devastating. The path I had been taught—school, job, work hard—wasn't leading to the financial freedom I craved.

I asked a professor, "How can we make more money as new grad physical therapists?" His response: "Joses, this is a helping profession. It's not about the money." This led to one of my biggest emotional crashes. My grades plummeted, and I felt hopeless, trapped in a suffocating situation with no escape.

I remember being in tears on my girlfriend's couch (who is now my wife). I felt like an imposter, stuck in a shrinking box that I could not escape. One of my lowest evenings was during the fall in Michigan where I went to school. The leaves had started to fall off, and you could hear the crackling in the branches because they were bare. I felt hopeless. I could barely see anything as the tears of frustration and confusion built up in my eyes. I could hear the wind just outside her living room window. I could still taste the late cup of coffee I had just finished. I could smell the banana bread that hadn't been touched because my appetite had completely left me. This would be my life, and there was nothing I could do about it. Everything I had wanted to run away from had caught up with me. The three things I wanted for myself and my future family seemingly did not exist. The one thing I had been chasing was not going to be possible. I felt just like that 10-year-old kid stuck in the elevator, trapped with no way out.

I went from being a focused, locked-in, excited, strong student to nearly leaving the school I was at, to nearly giving up on everything. My professors were concerned because they saw such a drastic drop in my performance. I almost threw everything away—all the sacrifices my parents had made, the years I had put into this focused dream—down the drain because I couldn't solve this problem: how to make sure this didn't financially feel like a trap. And I don't want this to happen to you. This is why the conversation we will have over the next few chapters is so important.

Reflect On Setbacks:

- Have you ever experienced a significant setback or realization that made you question your chosen path?
- How did you respond, and what did you learn from it?

Millionaire Mentor

Everything changed for me a few months later when my current business partner, but peer at the time, and good friend, Casey Coleman, introduced me to a man who changed my life. This man was Greg Todd, a "millionaire physical therapist." He became the key to the problem I felt I couldn't get out of, to the trap I had fallen into, to this cage I didn't think could be escaped from. No other physical therapist, no other professional, no one in my family, no professors I had could help me see a way out. Greg became the key to that.

Casey, who was a year behind me in physical therapy school, was posting blogs online. I was curious and asked him, "What are you doing? Is that what they're teaching you in school now?" He said, "No, no, no. They're not teaching us that in school. I hired a mentor, Greg Todd, and he's been teaching me how to use the knowledge I currently have to serve people who could use it online."

I was mind-blown. We planned a meeting on our campus, and Casey showed me everything. He said, "Joses, what if you just learn how to take the small Pre-PT mentorship project that we've been doing on campus for free, and become the go-to for that? Not just on our campus, but in the country. And we just learn from my mentor how to turn that skill into a business that can actually make us money."

I was in. I was locked in. I knew that if I modeled success, used a proven strategy, and had someone who had been there before and done that before, I could be successful, even though I was still a student. I hired that millionaire PT as my first mentor as well. I took something I was already good at—helping students get into grad school—and learned how to impact many more students with it, beyond our campus. It was through this journey that I realized the value of mentorship, a core principle we instill in our Impact to Income University coaching program.

That unlocked our first of several moneymakers. For us, a moneymaker is synonymous with a business or a set of skills or gifts that you can use to serve people online. It's a mix between an online business and an online side hustle. That first moneymaker still makes us hundreds of thousands of dollars each year and has allowed us to generate over seven figures. It's allowed my family—my wife and two kids—to live minutes from the ocean in Florida, which has been a dream for us as two Midwest-raised kids as well as an immigrant.

Path to Freedom

> **"The secret of getting ahead is getting started."**
> **— Mark Twain**

This chapter is about the journey from feeling trapped to finding freedom. It's about realizing that no one is coming to save you—you have to save yourself. It's about creating a unified vision for your life and taking control of your destiny.

Create Your Freedom Plan:

Define Your Vision: Write a detailed description of what financial freedom, time, and flexibility look like for you. Be as specific as possible.
Identify Obstacles: List the major obstacles that are currently preventing you from achieving your vision. Be honest and thorough.

Action Steps: For each obstacle, brainstorm at least two action steps you can take to overcome it. These steps should be practical and achievable.

1.
2.
3.
4.
5.

Timeline: Create a timeline for implementing your action steps. Set realistic deadlines for each step and include milestones to track your progress. Use a separate paper or notes at end of chapter if you need more space.
Commitment Statement: Write a commitment statement that outlines your dedication to achieving your vision. Sign and date it as a personal contract with yourself

Let's reflect on this journey. We've explored how fear of being trapped shaped my life and the importance of taking control of your destiny. Wondering what's next? It's time to tackle the myths that keep us trapped. In Chapter 2, we'll dissect the myth that working harder automatically leads to more money and uncover the truth behind real wealth creation.

Are you ready to start your journey toward real financial freedom? Let's dive into Chapter 2 and transform the way you think about money, work, and success. Trust me, you won't want to put this book down.

NOTES

NOTES

NOTES

NOTES

CHAPTER 2

The Hard Work Myth

Chapter 2

The Hard Work Myth

Why Working Smarter Beats Working Harder

Remember being told, "Just work hard, and you'll be successful"? It's a mantra drilled into us by parents, teachers, and society. But here's the kicker: It's not entirely true. Working hard is great, but the real question is: Are you working hard at the right things?

"It's not about how hard you work. It's about how smart you work."
— Unknown

Think back to a time when you had a job, or maybe even your current job, where you felt you should have been paid more. Why is that? Most people would say, "I gave it my all. I worked really hard, showed up early, did more than I was asked, and was a good team player." But despite all that effort, the paycheck didn't match the hard work. Sound familiar?

While it's good to work hard, it doesn't guarantee more money. This is a tough pill to swallow because it's the opposite of what most of us have been taught. Working hard at the right things is what equals success, not just working hard alone. In a moment, you'll uncover how this ties into the idea of low-dollar, middle-dollar, and high-dollar skills.

Income Analysis Activity

Create a list of all the jobs you've had and categorize them into low-dollar, middle-dollar, and high-dollar skills. Reflect on the tasks and skills required for each job and how they impacted your earnings.

Breaking Old Chains

To really get this, let me share what I've picked up over the last decade. It all comes down to understanding how more money is actually made, typically in three stages—the three levels of income. Many of us don't realize it, but we've been conditioned to think that working harder or going to more school automatically leads to success. This belief comes from our upbringing and the education system. I'll explain more in a bit, but let me be clear: that's not how it works anymore.

There was a time when this was true. The advice from our parents—more school equals more money—worked decades ago. But we're in a different era now. I'm sure you've noticed it. Maybe you've thought, "I'm spending all this time and money on schooling, but someone at a restaurant can climb to management and earn as much, if not more, without the debt and extra years of education."

We've all noticed these things, felt a bit suspicious, but didn't know what to do with that information. That's what I want you to understand. In fact, those who work the hardest physically and have the most demanding jobs often make the least money. This isn't a political statement; it's just how things work. In a moment, I will explain why.

I learned this firsthand working my first job at the same grocery store my parents had worked at when we first immigrated to the U.S. While that job was the least amount of money I have ever made working, it was also the hardest I have ever had to physically work for money.

Personal Experience Reflection

- Think about a time when you worked extremely hard but felt underpaid. What tasks did you perform, and why do you think the compensation didn't match your effort?
- How did this experience shape your view on hard work and money?

Facing Truth

> "The truth will set you free, but first it will piss you off."
> — Gloria Steinem

That quote perfectly describes what you're about to experience, not just in this chapter but throughout this book. While this book might indeed piss you off at times, understanding that this discomfort is a necessary step toward real financial freedom is crucial.

Now, let's dive into the three levels of income: low-dollar skills, middle-dollar skills, and high-dollar skills. What I'm about to share with you might flip everything you think you know about money, jobs, and wealth upside down. It certainly did for me. For the first time, I finally understood why making more money always seemed impossible and why it was so frustrating to see

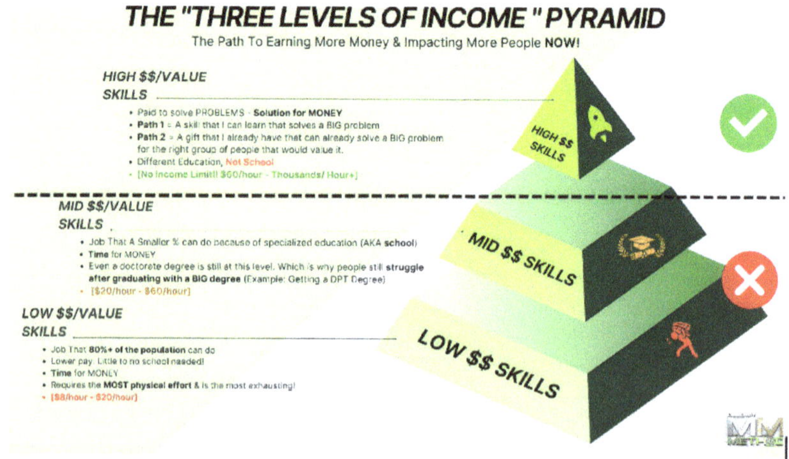

those I loved work so hard physically but have very little to show for it.

Once you grasp this, it will change the game for you.

Low-Dollar Skills

Low-dollar skills are jobs most people can do. They need little to no special education and are all about trading time for money. They're physically exhausting and offer the lowest pay. For example, think about who works the hardest in a hotel—it's usually the individuals cleaning the rooms. They're also the ones paid the least because their skills are easily replaceable.

These jobs typically pay from minimum wage up to about $20 an hour. If you're in a job like this and trying to make more money, it seems nearly impossible because it means working more hours and becoming even more exhausted.

Middle-Dollar Skills

Next up, middle-dollar skills. These jobs need specialized education, so fewer people can do them. This includes professions like lawyers, physical therapists, or any job that requires graduate school or special certifications. You're still trading time for money, but you're paid more because fewer people can do these jobs.

Even though these professions might seem like the pinnacle of success, they often cap out at middle-dollar skills. For example, a physical therapist might make between $20 and $60 an hour, but when you factor in student debt and the rising cost of living, it's easy to feel stuck. You've invested so much time and money into your education, but the financial returns don't always add up.

Belief Assessment

- What beliefs about hard work and success were instilled in you growing up?
- How have these beliefs influenced your career choices and financial decisions?

High-Dollar Skills

Here's where it gets exciting. High-dollar skills are where true wealth kicks in. These skills aren't necessarily harder to acquire but require a shift in how you think about work and money. The key difference is that high-dollar skills pay you to solve problems, not just for your time. You're providing solutions for money, and this changes everything.

"The future belongs to those who learn more skills and combine them in creative ways." – Robert Greene

There are two paths to uncovering high-dollar skills:

1. **Learning a Skill that Solves a Big Problem:** The bigger the problem you solve, the more money you can make. This is a massive shift from what we know from school, where we're taught that time is money. In reality, time is infinitely more valuable than money.

2. **Using a Gift You Already Have to Solve an Existing Problem:** This is what we'll focus on in this book. It's about finding and mastering your moneymaker—a gift you already possess that can solve a significant problem for others. When you can use your gift to solve problems, the financial rewards can be substantial.

Reprogram for Success

- Is it possible we've been programmed to think that working hard and going to more school is the only or best way to succeed? And that anyone who does it differently is wrong, greedy, or lucky?

- Reflect on how your education and upbringing might have influenced your beliefs about work and money.

School System's Influence

The school system has been set up this way on purpose. John D. Rockefeller, who founded the General Education Board in 1902, is attributed to saying, "I don't want a nation of thinkers, I want a nation of workers."

"Formal education will make you a living; self-education will make you a fortune." — Jim Rohn

From the beginning, school was designed to make us good at following instructions, not thinking for ourselves. This system creates good employees who work hard for a fraction of someone else's money. Most people end up working 40 hours a week, begging for a few vacation days, and hoping for a small raise. This is the world of low-dollar and middle-dollar skills.

You've been led to believe that high-dollar skills are out of reach, but the education system was designed to keep you as a worker, not a thinker. One book that opened my eyes to this was "Weapons of Mass Instruction." It uncovered many beliefs that were holding me back.

The Shift to High-Dollar Skills

Now, imagine breaking free from this conditioning. What if you could play at the high-dollar skill level, using your unique gifts to solve problems and create significant value? You don't need more school; you need to learn to work hard at the right things.

We have students who, while still in school, are making more money than seasoned professionals. They've learned to play the game differently, focusing on high-dollar skills. Here's a success story from one of our Impact To Income University Coaching clients, Joel:

Joel's Journey to High-Dollar Skills

"My biggest perspective change was understanding the principles behind the pieces that go into playing at the high-dollar skills level and into a moneymaker, and really understanding how those things work together. In the last five months, I've been able to put together an offer and reach five to six paying clients. The opportunities are endless. A huge shout-out to Joses, Casey, and their team for all they do. They know how to approach each step, and it's been great to be part of this community and see the impact of these skills beyond just healthcare."

So, do you want to keep playing the game of working hard for more money, or do you want to learn to work hard at the right things and make exponentially more? If you're ready to uncover your high-dollar skills and change your financial future, keep reading. This book will guide you through the process of finding and developing your moneymaker.

Transforming Money Beliefs

In this chapter, we've busted the myth that hard work alone brings in more money. We've uncovered the truth behind low-dollar, middle-dollar, and high-dollar skills. Now, you might be wondering, "What's next?" The next step is crucial—questioning and reshaping your beliefs about money.

Read and Reflect Activity

- Read a book or an article about the changing landscape of work and how different skills are valued. Reflect on how this new information aligns or conflicts with your current beliefs about hard work and success.

In Chapter 3, we'll delve into the power of beliefs. Have you ever considered that the beliefs you hold about money could be the very things holding you back? We'll explore how our upbringing, society, and personal experiences shape our financial beliefs and how those beliefs impact our ability to make more money.

Are you ready to challenge your current mindset and adopt new, empowering beliefs that align with your financial goals? In the next chapter, we'll dive deep into questioning and transforming your money beliefs, setting the foundation for building your moneymaker. Let's continue this journey together and unlock your true potential.

NOTES

NOTES

NOTES

NOTES

CHAPTER 3

Rewrite Your Money Story

Chapter 3

Rewrite Your Money Story

Transforming Limiting Beliefs into Empowering Wealth Mindsets

Beliefs Matter

"A lie believed as truth will affect your life as if it were true." — Craig Groeschel, *Winning the War in Your Mind*

Have you ever wondered if your beliefs about wealth and money are the walls blocking you from earning more and impacting more people? What if the beliefs we've held since childhood aren't serving us now? If you've had a fantastic environment where your money beliefs have served you well, that's amazing. But this chapter is for those who haven't had that experience.

Our beliefs often come from well-meaning parents, teachers, and society. These beliefs shape our financial reality and can hold us back. Before we go any further, let's question those beliefs and see if they truly serve us. Because if they don't, it's going to be hard to apply anything else you learn in this book. Beliefs shape our actions, and actions shape our results. If we want more money, our money beliefs are directly connected to that. Would you agree? Let's dive in.

Your Money Story

Pause for a moment. Think about your earliest memories of money. What did the influential people in your life teach you? This could be your parents, guardians, relatives, teachers, or even friends. Do any of these sound familiar?

- "More money is selfish."
- "I don't want to be greedy."
- "Money can't buy happiness."
- "I can't help people now, maybe in five to ten years."
- "I'm too busy; I don't have time."

"Your money beliefs drive your money behaviors."
— Suze Orman

Reflect & Write:

Take a moment to jot down your earliest memory of money. Write a short paragraph about a specific incident that shaped your initial beliefs about money.

These beliefs aren't necessarily true; they're perspectives that can either empower you or hold you back. Let's unpack them together.

My Old Beliefs

More Money is Selfish

Many of us were taught that wanting more money is selfish. But think about it: money is a tool. It can be used for selfish purposes, but it can also help others, create opportunities, and make a positive impact. When you earn more, you have more resources to give back. It's not the money that's selfish; it's how you choose to use it.

Reflect & Reframe:

- Do you believe that wanting more money is selfish? Why or why not?
- Write down one way you could reframe this belief into something positive and empowering.

I Don't Want to Be Greedy

This belief often stems from the misconception that having more means taking away from others. But the economy is not a zero-sum game. Creating wealth can generate more opportunities and resources for others. It's about creating value, not taking it away.

Money Can't Buy Happiness

Sure, money can't buy happiness, but it can provide security, freedom, and the ability to make choices that enhance your quality of life. It can fund experiences, support loved ones, and create a safety net.

I Can't Help People Now

You don't need to wait until you're wealthy to help others. Small acts of kindness and generosity can have a ripple effect. Plus, the skills and resources you develop while building your wealth can amplify your ability to help others in the future.

I'm Too Busy, I Don't Have Time

We all have the same 24 hours in a day. It's about how you use them. Leveraging your time effectively, prioritizing tasks, and focusing on high-impact activities can create more time for what matters most.

My New Beliefs

Now, let's replace those old, limiting beliefs with new, empowering ones:

- **More Money, More Impact:** The more money you make, the more you can give back, support causes you care about, and create opportunities for others.
- **Creating Value Isn't Greedy:** By solving problems and creating value, you're contributing to society and earning your fair share.
- **Money as a Tool for Good:** Money can enhance your life and the lives of others. It's a means to an end, not the end itself.
- **Helping Now and Later:** You can make a difference now, and as you grow your wealth, your capacity to help will also grow.

- **Efficient Use of Time:** Leverage your time by focusing on high-value activities and delegating or automating low-value tasks.

"Change your thoughts and you change your world." — Norman Vincent Peale

Life Shaped by Beliefs

Beliefs are everything. Every decision you make, every action you take, comes back to what you believe. Your beliefs shape your life. So, if we're going to learn how to impact more people and generate more income, doesn't it make sense to examine the beliefs we hold about making money and helping others?

When I started this journey, my beliefs weren't serving me. Many were tied to how I grew up. For this book to transform your life, your beliefs must align with the strategies we'll discuss. If they don't, no amount of information will help. As Myron Golden teaches, there are three levels to achieving any outcome. First, you need to become the person who can achieve it. Then, you need to do the things that lead to the outcome. Finally, you'll have the result you desire.

Becoming "the Person"

Becoming means adopting beliefs that align with the results you want and developing the skills to get there. Once you become the person who has the right beliefs and mindset, you'll feel empowered to take the necessary actions. This is crucial because many people make the mistake of thinking that all they need is more information. But information alone isn't enough.

Think back to a time when you had all the information you needed, but it still didn't work out. Maybe it was a book you read, a YouTube video you watched, or a podcast you listened to. Your brain tricked you into thinking you didn't know enough yet to act. This turns you into an information junkie—consuming content but never applying it. Why? Because you haven't become the person who can take action. The beliefs and mindset come first.

Look Back & Reflect:

- Reflect on a time when you had all the information you needed but still didn't take action. What held you back?
- Write a few sentences about what you believe stopped you from acting.

____

____

____

____

The Power of Action

Doing the right things repeatedly leads to the outcomes you want. If your goal is to make more money, then becoming the person with the right beliefs is the first step. The second step is consistently taking the right actions. Without aligning your beliefs with your goals, you'll remain stuck, no matter how much information you gather.

"The secret of getting ahead is getting started."
— Mark Twain

Set Your Goals:

- Set one short-term and one long-term financial goal. What actions will you take to achieve these goals?

SHORT TERM	LONG TERM

- What beliefs do you need to adopt to support your actions?

Evaluating Your Beliefs

So, what are your current beliefs about money? Do they align with making more impact and income? If not, it's time to analyze and challenge those beliefs. Ask yourself if they're serving you. If not, consider adopting new beliefs that align with where you want to go.

Belief Evaluation:

1. **Reflect on Your Beliefs:** Write down your current beliefs about money. Be honest with yourself.

___

___

___

2. **Analyze the Origin:** Where did these beliefs come from? Parents? Teachers? Society?

___

___

___

3. **Challenge the Beliefs:** Are these beliefs serving you? If not, how can you reframe them into empowering beliefs?

___

___

___

4. **Adopt New Beliefs:** Replace old beliefs with new ones that support your financial goals and values.

___

___

___

My Transformation

A lot of my early beliefs about money were shaped by my upbringing. I grew up in a religious environment where money was commonly believed to be the root of all evil. This belief stems from the biblical scripture that says, "For the love of money is the root of all evil" (1 Timothy 6:10). I can also remember hearing and reading passages like, "It is easier for a camel to go through the eye of a needle than for a rich man to enter the kingdom of heaven" (Matthew 19:24). Although these are biblically accurate verses, I later learned and understood that many of these passages are taken out of context. However, initially, they led me to believe that wealth was inherently bad and that poverty was somehow virtuous.

As I grew older, especially during my second year of PT school, and met various people over the last ten years, I started to question these beliefs. I noticed that not all wealthy people were greedy or evil, as movies and shows often portrayed. My first mentor, who I shared about earlier in this book, was a millionaire and a physical therapist. But character-wise, he was the exact opposite of what I had seen in movies. He was kind, a family man, deeply spiritual, and extremely giving. The people I met later on further challenged my negative beliefs about wealth and those who were wealthy.

If I resist something and truly believe it is bad, I won't allow myself to embrace it. This challenged a lot of my previous notions about money and wealth. A book that profoundly impacted me and gave me more context and perspective was *Business Secrets from the Bible* by Rabbi Daniel Lapin. This book helped me reframe my understanding of money and wealth. It made me realize that money is a massively powerful tool, even a spiritual tool. The way you leverage it is everything. The activities you do to generate more income, like high-dollar skills, require you to bless and impact more people and solve bigger problems.

We have to separate evil people and greedy people on both ends of the wealth spectrum from the actual tool itself, which is money. I believe that money is inherently good. Along this journey, I saw examples of wealthy biblical figures like Solomon and how their wealth was acquired. There were success principles that worked then and still work now. Myron Golden has stated that his entire business is built on the principles Solomon used. Seeing individuals who align with my core beliefs and values helped me unlearn the negative, scarcity-based perceptions I had about money and wealth.

The more I challenged those beliefs, the more I opened myself up to earning more and blessing more people. This shift in perspective, much like the one our Impact to Income University coaching clients experience, allowed me to see money as a tool for good—a way to create value and make a positive impact. It was when I started to shift my direction and perception of generational wealth and legacy that I truly began to see the potential for my future and my family's future.

I began to ask myself questions like, "If more money is bad, where does it come from?" and "How can I use my gifts to create value for others?" This process of questioning and challenging my beliefs led to significant shifts in my mindset and my approach to money.

Mindset To Millions

Daymond John's journey from humble beginnings to entrepreneurial success is a powerful example of how changing your mindset can transform your financial future. Growing up in Queens, New York, Daymond faced numerous challenges, including limited financial resources and a tough neighborhood. However, he didn't let these obstacles define his future.

Daymond's entrepreneurial journey began with a simple idea: he noticed a gap in the market for affordable, stylish streetwear. With his mother's support, he started FUBU (For Us, By Us) from their home. Daymond and his friends sewed hats and shirts themselves, initially selling them on the streets of New York.

Despite having to work a full-time job to fund his business, Daymond persisted. His big break came when LL Cool J, a popular rapper at the time, wore a FUBU hat in a commercial. This exposure catapulted FUBU into mainstream success, eventually turning it into a multi-million dollar brand.

Daymond's story doesn't end there. He became one of the original investors on the television show *Shark Tank*, where he now helps aspiring entrepreneurs realize their dreams. His journey illustrates how shifting your beliefs about money—from seeing it as a barrier to viewing it as a tool for achieving great things—can lead to extraordinary success. Daymond's story shows that with determination, innovation, and the right mindset, anyone can transform their financial reality and make a lasting impact.

Client Stories

- **Ashley's Shift:** Ashley was raised with a biblical understanding of money, learning early on that money is a tool for sowing rather than hoarding. Her father's teachings emphasized saving for the purpose of giving, and she was also introduced to the concept of leverage from a young age. However, these principles only truly resonated with her during a challenging season in her life. Inspired by teachings on resourcefulness and leveraging relationships, Ashley began to see the abundance of resources and connections around her. Today, Ashley is the owner and founder of the Baylor Strong Project, where she supports families through pancreatic cancer. As a student, she has built a platform and community for caregivers, providing guidance, resources, and hope. Ashley's business not only generates exponential impact for her community and her family but also allows her to truly apply the principles she has embodied in her journey. Her transformation highlights the impact of leveraging resources and embracing a growth mindset.
- **Joel's Transformation:** Joel grew up with the belief that hard work alone was the key to financial success. Influenced by his grandparents' dedication and his parents' continuous learning, he pursued a traditional career path in medicine. However, Joel's mindset began to shift when he realized the power of leveraging skills beyond a regular job. He started filming for a high school football

team and quickly saw the impact of his work on players' futures. This experience taught him the value of skill-based work and creating opportunities. Today, Joel is the owner of CAA Loading, where he coaches pre-CAA students, helping them get accepted into grad schools. He is successfully generating income without trading his time for money. Joel's journey from a traditional mindset to embracing skill-based income is a testament to the transformative power of shifting money beliefs.

- **Alejandro's Transformation:** Alejandro grew up in a family of five, where his immigrant parents viewed money as scarce and limited. He was taught to make money last by avoiding luxury items and focusing on daily essentials. Education was highly valued, and Alejandro believed that more education equated to more money. However, his mindset began to shift over time. Inspired by new teachings and the concept of providing value through skills and serving his audience, Alejandro realized that income is linked to the value you bring. Today, Alejandro is the owner of SpanishPhysio, where he teaches clinicians Spanish so they can effectively treat and serve their patients even without a translator. Alejandro's journey from a scarcity mindset to a value-driven approach highlights the power of shifting beliefs and embracing new perspectives.

Closing Thoughts

Shifting your money beliefs is crucial to building a successful moneymaker and creating a life of abundance. Remember, a belief that doesn't serve you can hold you back. It's time to question those beliefs, embrace new ones, and unlock your true potential.

Your Move:

- **Develop an Action Plan:** Create a step-by-step plan to start implementing new, empowering beliefs about money. This plan should include small daily actions you can take to reinforce these new beliefs.

Try This: Belief Journaling

- Spend 10 minutes each day for a week writing down any thoughts or feelings about money that come up during your day. At the end of the week, review your entries to identify patterns or recurring themes.

Try This: Visualization Exercise

- Visualize your ideal financial future. What does it look like? How do you feel? Who are you helping with your wealth? Write down this vision in detail, focusing on every aspect of your ideal financial life.

Up Next

As we conclude this chapter, take a moment to reflect on the beliefs you've challenged and the new ones you're ready to embrace. This is the foundation for everything that follows. The next chapter will delve into finding your perfect moneymaker—identifying and developing the unique gifts and skills that will propel you to financial freedom. The journey of self-discovery and financial empowerment continues. Are you ready to uncover what your moneymaker is? Let's dive in.

NOTES

NOTES

NOTES

NOTES

CHAPTER 4

Unlock Your Unique Moneymaker

Chapter 4

Unlocking Your Unique Moneymaker

Turning Hidden Talents into Profitable Ventures

Uncover Your Gift

Now that we've spent some time challenging and potentially shifting our beliefs about money, are you ready to uncover what your moneymaker is? At this point, most of our clients are typically excited about the possibility of going down a new path that can allow them to bless more people and generate more money. But their biggest question is, what is "my thing"? This is the key difference between feeling like everything in this book is possible for others versus feeling like this is actually possible for you, right now. How many times have we fallen into the trap of believing that something like this is possible for others but not for ourselves? We trick ourselves into believing that other people have an advantage that we don't.

This chapter is going to be extremely important. We're going to uncover what your gift is and show you how you can turn that gift into money. The best part is that you already have it inside of you; we just need to help you pull it out. In our community with our coaching clients, we call that a moneymaker. To keep it simple, a moneymaker is unlocked when we uncover skills and gifts that you already have and link them to an existing problem that other people have and would pay to have solved. This process allows you to turn those skills and gifts into money online.

"Everyone has a purpose, and when you find it, you'll unlock your full potential." — Anonymous

The beauty of this approach is that it leverages your current strengths. No need to learn something brand new. You already have what it takes. We just need to connect your skills to a problem people are eager to solve. That's where the magic happens. People pay to have their problems solved. You using your gift to solve these problems is where the money is created. The bigger the problem, the bigger the reward. We'll dive deeper into the money aspect in Chapter 5. But for now, let's uncover your moneymaker. Are you ready?

Your Inner Moneymaker

This chapter is all about helping you start getting ideas and hopefully locking in on potential things you can do for others in exchange for money. I want you to see that this is actually possible for you, wherever you're currently at in your life. This is possible for you.

**"Your talent is God's gift to you. What you do with it is your gift back to God."
— Leo Buscaglia**

The reason why this chapter might be one of the most important ones you've read so far, and may even read in this book, is because this chapter will allow you to unlock the belief that you can help more people now. But also the belief that you can find and solve a big enough problem that others would be willing to pay for using the things you're already good at. It's the belief that everyone has one of these.

When we see someone who's successful, we often assume they have an advantage we don't. The truth is, they just know how to use the gifts and skills they already have, and they know how to exchange those to provide enough value and solve enough problems to generate a lot of income. I want to show you how realistic that is for you right now.

Chisel Your Genius

Think of yourself as a sculptor, and your talents and skills are a block of marble. At first glance, the marble may seem like just a solid, unremarkable block. But a skilled sculptor knows that within that block lies a beautiful statue waiting to be revealed. The sculptor doesn't add anything to the marble; instead, they chisel away the excess to uncover the masterpiece within. Similarly, you already possess the skills and talents needed to create your moneymaker. It's not about adding new capabilities; it's about chiseling away doubts and distractions to reveal the valuable skills you already have. Just as a sculptor reveals a statue from marble, you will uncover your moneymaker by focusing on what you already excel at and finding a way to apply it to solve problems for others.

> **"Every block of stone has a statue inside it and it is the task of the sculptor to discover it."**
> **— Michelangelo**

Skill Reflection:

Take a moment to think about the people you admire. What skills or gifts do they use to create value? Jot down a few names and their talents. Now, think about yourself—what talents do you have that might not seem obvious but could be incredibly valuable?

For example, we didn't realize we had a moneymaker when we started helping students on our campus for free. We were helping them prepare for grad school while we were still in undergrad. We'd figured out a few things that we thought were helpful and didn't realize that would ultimately become our first moneymaker. Some of the things you might not even realize are blessings or strengths can be some of the biggest aha moments for you.

Finding your moneymaker is like finding your golden door to the impact, life, and income that you've always dreamed about. This is what sets you apart from the 95% of the world. This is what will change everything for you once we do it correctly.

Joseph's Near Mistake

Let me share a story about one of our current clients who didn't internalize the fact that he had gifts already. You might be tempted to resist the idea that you have gifts, but I'm going to take you through an exercise to show you how to unlock those strengths and gifts right now.

Joseph attended one of our live events in 2023. He flew down to Tampa, Florida, where our event was, and we were teaching them this concept of the moneymaker and how every single person has a moneymaker. Part of him wanted to believe it, but he struggled to see how he could use the things he was already great at to solve an existing problem.

Joseph wanted to start an online business, but he felt like he didn't have something of value to provide the world. He thought about learning AI and using it to serve other businesses, but he had no experience with AI. I asked him, "Why are you going down a path where you have zero experience or strengths?" He said he didn't feel like he had any gifts.

So, we went through a process of uncovering his gifts and strengths. Joseph is a triathlete and loved helping new triathletes. He realized that he could help new triathletes complete a half or full Ironman without injury or regret. That was his lightbulb moment. He had a legitimate moneymaker—something he was already great at, and he could help people with right now. Joseph is now the owner of Morphit Physical Therapy & Sports Performance, where he helps endurance athletes dominate their training and races.

Your Unique Gifts

Just like Joseph, you have a gift or a set of skills that, if we learn how to uncover them, you could unlock an online money-making machine, also known as a moneymaker. Don't be deceived by looking at what others are doing and assuming that's the only way. You are unique. You have been designed and crafted differently from every other human being on earth. Why not tap into your unique experiences and strengths?

Before we dive into the process of uncovering your moneymaker, there's a perspective shift we need to embrace. This perspective shift is crucial. It will enable you to see yourself as someone who can genuinely use what you're about to uncover in the next sections and bring it to life.

Perspective Shift: I Am a Problem Solver

To unlock your moneymaker, we need to change our identity. We must shift from seeing ourselves as just a student, new grad, or employee, to seeing ourselves as problem solvers. The people who get paid the most, especially with moneymakers, are those who solve problems. If you see yourself as just an employee or student, it's going to be hard to see yourself as someone who can pull this off.

Mindset Affirmation:

Start saying to yourself, "I am a problem solver." Repeat it daily. Write it down and place it somewhere visible. This mindset shift will help you think like a problem solver and find ways to take your gifts and solve problems for others. People pay for solutions, and this activity will help you find your moneymaker. In fact, many of our Impact to Income University coaching clients have discovered their unique moneymakers through this very process.

The Moneymaker Formula

Here's the moneymaker formula:

Personal Strengths and Desires + Relevant and Growing Problem + Create Solution = My Moneymaker

Let's break this down with four questions that will help you uncover your moneymaker.

Step-by-Step: Uncovering Your Moneymaker

Question 1: What Do You Love to Do?

Identify your passions and interests—the activities and subjects that make you lose track of time because you're so consumed in them. What excites you to wake up in the morning? Take five minutes, set a timer, play some music, and write down the answers.

Discover Your Passions:

Make a list of at least 10 things you love to do and 10 things you are good at doing. Set a timer for 10 minutes and write freely without overthinking.

Purpose: To help you identify your passions and strengths, which are the foundation of your moneymaker.

Question 2: What Are You Good at Doing?

Think about the skills and talents you have right now. What do people celebrate you for? What do your friends and family members say you're great at? These are your skills and talents. Take five minutes to write down the list.

Question 3: What Problems Does Your Community Have?

Reflect on problems you've noticed locally and online. What are some problems you've seen that you could help solve? If you're unsure, I'll show you how to leverage AI to help you uncover these problems.

Identify Community Needs:

Spend 15 minutes observing your community (either online or offline) and jot down at least 5 problems you notice people facing. These could be issues discussed in forums, social media, or even in your local neighborhood.

Purpose: To identify real-world problems that you can solve with your unique skills and talents.

Question 4: What Will People Pay For?

Think about what people are willing to spend money on. People pay for more time, convenience, clarity, and direction. What would people pay for that aligns with what you're good at and what you love to do? Take five minutes to write down your thoughts.

Leveraging AI to Find Problems and Solutions

If you're stuck on questions 3 and 4, you can leverage AI to help. At the time of writing this, ChatGPT is the most accessible option, but there are others available, like Google's Bard, OpenAI's Codex, and Jasper AI. Depending on when you're reading this, be aware of the different options. As long as the AI can execute what I'm about to share, use it.

Here's a prompt you can use:

> "I am currently in the process of identifying problems that I can solve that people would pay money for, specifically online. I will give you a list of the things I love to do and the things I'm good at doing. Please provide an extensive list of real problems that people are looking for solutions to, which align with my strengths and interests."

Once you have a list of problems, you can ask the AI to provide a list of solutions people would pay for:

> "Based on the problems identified and my strengths and interests, what are some solutions people would be willing to pay for?"

AI-Powered Brainstorming:

Use an AI tool like ChatGPT to help you brainstorm problems and solutions. Input your list of things you love to do and are good at doing, and ask the AI to suggest problems you can solve and potential solutions.

Purpose: To leverage technology in uncovering opportunities that align with your strengths.

Bringing It All Together

Now, it's time to piece it all together. Go back to AI and use this prompt:

> "I will give you my answers to four questions. Please provide five perfectly aligned online business ideas that would leverage my current strengths and skills, solve real problems that people are willing to pay for, and have a growing audience."

Input your answers to the four questions and see what the AI provides. Repeat this process until you have one to three potential moneymakers.

Map Out Your Moneymaker:

Take a piece of paper or open a digital mind-mapping tool. In the center, write "My Moneymaker." Create branches for each of the four questions and fill in your answers. This visual representation will help you see connections and potential ideas more clearly.

Challenge: Discover Your Moneymaker in 7 Days

I challenge you to identify your moneymaker within the next seven days. Dedicate time each day to reflect, write down ideas, and use the AI prompts. By the end of the week, you'll have a clearer vision of your moneymaker and be ready to take the next steps.

Believe in Your Unique Potential

Remember, you have unique gifts and strengths that no one else has. Believe in your potential to solve problems and create value. This journey is about unlocking what's already inside you. Trust the process and stay committed. You are capable of achieving more than you ever imagined.

Steps to Success

Now that you've gone through the visualization exercise and discovered your moneymaker, you're well on your way to unlocking your potential. Trust the process, stay committed, and remember, you are capable of achieving more than you've ever imagined.

Before we transition into Chapter 5, where we'll dive into how to make money and turn your moneymaker idea into real income, there's one crucial concept to understand. This idea will set the foundation for the success you're about to experience.

More Problems, More Money?

One thing that the wealthiest people I've learned from have internalized is this: more problems equal more money. We've discussed how making money using a moneymaker, an online business, or just business in general, involves getting paid to solve problems. In the next chapter, we'll dive deeper into this concept. But for now, I need you to start understanding this fundamental principle: more problems, more money?

The best in this game love solving problems. Over the years of doing this and teaching this, I've learned that there are three types of people: problem creators, problem avoiders, and problem solvers. My question to you is, which one do you mostly show up as?

- **Problem Creators:** These individuals are typically victims and complainers. They blame others for their situation and look for others to save them.
- **Problem Avoiders:** This is a large group. They try to mind their own business and only focus on their situ-

ation. While this makes them good citizens, it doesn't solve their problems.

- **Problem Solvers:** The wealthiest people I know fall into this category. They see problems as opportunities and actively seek solutions.

During the 2020 pandemic, while many businesses struggled, ours grew by 2.5 times. This wasn't because we took advantage of anything. It was because people had problems, and we got creative in solving them. This mindset shift is crucial. As you figure out what your moneymaker is, decide to become a problem solver. Don't just obsess over your own situation; focus on how you can solve others' problems.

Remember, people pay to have their problems solved. As we move into Chapter 5, we'll explore how to make money—not just a little, but a lot. I'll share the process that has helped us generate over seven figures. You'll realize it's not as complicated as you think. The hardest part is not the "what to do," but becoming the person who can do it. It's about mastering the repetitions, just like you've done your entire life.

If you're ready to step into the role of a problem solver, then let's take your moneymaker ideas and dive into Chapter 5. We'll uncover the exact steps to turn this into actual money. Are you ready

NOTES

NOTES

NOTES

NOTES

CHAPTER 5

Profit From Your Passion

Chapter 5

Profit From Your Passion

Converting Free Value into Lucrative Income Streams

From Free to Paid

"Opportunities don't happen. You create them." — Chris Grosser

Now that you've identified your moneymaker, it's time to turn your passion and skills into actual money. In this chapter, we'll focus on transitioning from offering free value online to securing paying beta clients. Charging for your services, even at a beta price, ensures that your clients are invested and committed. This approach, often utilized by our Impact to Income University coaching clients, helps validate your moneymaker and boosts your confidence. This is the first step to validating your moneymaker and gaining confidence in your offer.

In a moment, you're about to unlock a five-step process that'll take you from serving people on your social media platform or online for free to getting five to ten of them to pay you as beta clients very soon. But first, let's understand what a beta is and why it's critical to boosting your confidence, making sure that you don't miss what your people want, and ensuring that you create an outcome they truly desire. This will prepare you to release this as a premium offer, which we will talk about in Chapter 6.

Beta Secrets

Picture this: a bustling university campus, a group of hopeful pre-physical therapy students, and a determined advisor telling them to give up on their dreams because of their low GPAs. This scene played out in front of my eyes, and it didn't sit right with me. How could someone with no experience in physical therapy dictate the futures of these students? It was a wake-up call, a moment that sparked a fire within me to create change.

Back then, Casey Coleman (my business partner) and I were just starting out. We knew there was a massive problem—students were being told they couldn't achieve their dreams because of a few grades. We had been helping our peers for free, guiding them to better grades and stronger applications. Our success was undeniable, but we hadn't thought about monetizing it yet. We were driven by a desire to help, not by profit.

We spent years serving students on our campus, answering their questions, and providing the support they desperately needed. It was fulfilling, but we realized this issue wasn't confined to our campus. Students everywhere were struggling, feeling hopeless and lost. We had to find a way to reach them.

Transitioning online was a leap of faith. For eight months, we offered free value through podcasts, live streams, and a Facebook group. We were determined to understand our audience better. The better you understand who you're helping, the better you can serve them. This understanding is crucial in creating programs that truly address their needs.

I remember it like it was yesterday. It was the fall of 2017, and Hurricane Irma was barreling towards Florida. My girlfriend (now wife) and I were evacuating, and I found myself in a McDonald's parking lot, about to go live on Facebook to announce our first beta program. The connection was terrible, the video was pixelated, but the message was clear. We were going to help students navigate their way from point A to point B over ten weeks.

We announced that we would take on ten beta clients, charging $250 each—a price that seemed astronomical at the time. But we did it. And to our surprise, ten people signed up. This beta program was a game-changer. It validated our approach, provided us with invaluable feedback, and gave us the confidence to continue.

From those humble beginnings, Pre-PT Grind has grown exponentially. We've helped thousands of students and generated over seven figures. The beta process was instrumental in our success. It confirmed that people were willing to pay for the solutions we offered and allowed us to refine our program based on real feedback.

Now, let's dive into the five steps that can help you turn your moneymaker into actual money, just as we did.

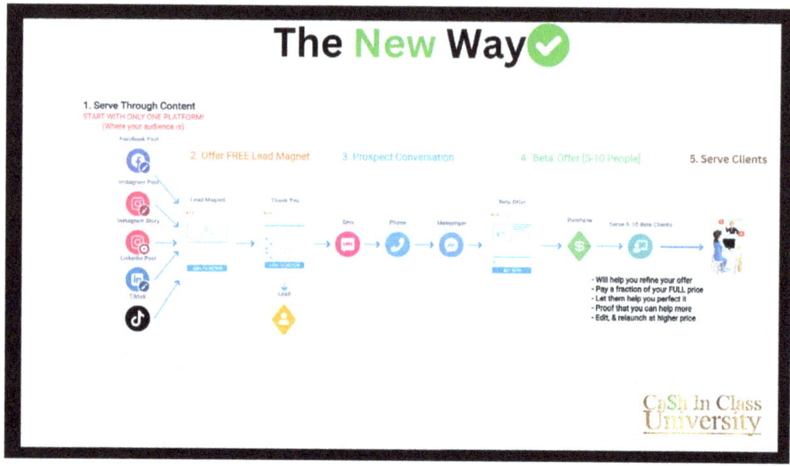

Five Steps to Money

Step 1: Content Creation – Serve Your Audience

Start by serving your audience with valuable content. The first step is to choose a platform where your audience hangs out. This could be Instagram, YouTube, Facebook, or any other platform where you know your potential clients are active. Next, create content that serves them—tips, tutorials, insights—anything that adds value and showcases your expertise.

Content Planning:

- Write down three content ideas. Use AI tools to help craft these ideas if necessary.

- Example: If you're targeting fitness enthusiasts, create content around workout tips, healthy recipes, and motivational stories. Engage with your audience using polls and questions.
- Reflection: What are three common questions your audience asks? Create content that directly answers these.

The key here is to build trust and establish yourself as an expert in your field. By consistently delivering valuable content, you create a relationship with your audience, making them more likely to invest in your beta offer.

Step 2: Lead Generation – Turn Attention into Contacts

Once you've established trust and built an audience, it's time to turn that attention into leads. Offer something valuable for free in exchange for contact information. This is known as a lead magnet. It could be a workout guide, a nutrition plan, a short video series, or anything else that provides immediate value to your audience.

Create a Lead Magnet:

- Draft an outline for a PDF guide addressing a common problem your audience faces. Use AI tools to design this guide.

- Example: Create a simple guide like "10 Tips to Improve Your Fitness Routine" or "A Beginner's Guide to Nutrition for Athletes."

The goal here is to collect contact information (usually email addresses) that you can use to nurture these leads through email marketing and other channels. This step is crucial because it allows you to build a database of potential clients who have already shown interest in what you offer.

Step 3: Engagement – Build Relationships

Now that you have leads, it's time to engage with them and build strong relationships. This involves more than just sending out automated emails. Engage with your audience through comments, messages, and interactive posts. Respond to their questions, acknowledge their feedback, and create a two-way conversation.

Lead Engagement:

- Write a script for your initial conversation with a lead. Practice engaging with them authentically and understanding their pain points.
- Example: If someone comments on your post about struggling with fitness, reply with a helpful tip and ask more about their challenges.

The more you engage, the more trust you build. And the more trust you build, the more likely these leads are to become paying clients. Building relationships increases trust and makes people more likely to invest in your beta offer.

Step 4: Offer Presentation – Launch Your Beta

Now it's time to present your beta offer. This can be done through direct messages, emails, or a dedicated landing page. The key is to highlight the benefits of your beta program and the exclusive opportunity for feedback. Make it clear that this is a unique chance for them to get personalized attention and contribute to the development of the final product.

Create Your Beta Offer:

- Create a simple landing page using a website builder. Include key points: problem you solve, benefits, and the feedback opportunity.
- Example: "Join my beta program to transform your fitness journey with personalized coaching. Limited spots available!"

Be sure to create a sense of urgency by emphasizing the limited spots and the exclusive nature of the beta program. This encourages potential clients to act quickly and secure their place.

"Feedback is the breakfast of champions."
— Ken Blanchard

Step 5: Deliver and Improve - Gather Feedback

Finally, deliver your beta program live and actively gather feedback from your participants. This feedback is invaluable as it allows you to make necessary adjustments and improvements to your offer. The goal is to refine your program based on real user experiences to ensure it meets the needs of your clients.

Collect and Act on Feedback:

- Develop a feedback form for your beta clients. Ask specific questions about their experience and desired improvements.
- Example: "What did you find most valuable about this program? What areas do you think need improvement?"

Use this feedback to continuously improve your program. Not only does this help you create a better product, but it also shows your clients that you value their input and are committed to providing the best possible service.

HOW TO BUILD YOUR BETA PROGRAM

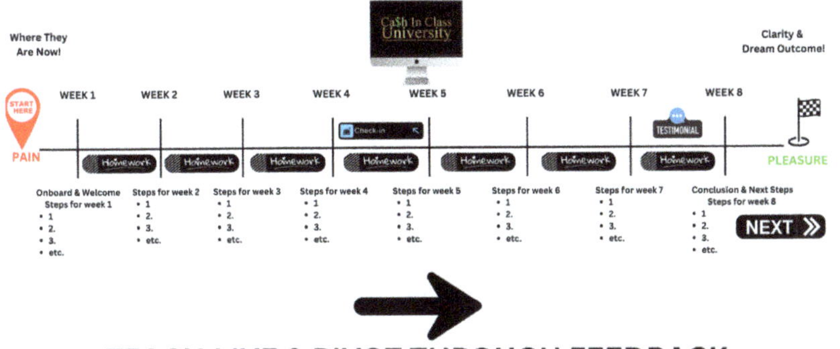

TEACH LIVE & PIVOT THROUGH FEEDBACK

Example: Robyn's Journey

One of our clients, Robyn, a Physiotherapist and Performance Coach, initially feared that the online space might not work for her. At the time, she had an in-person cash-based clinic and was feeling spread thin and overwhelmed because her main way of making money was treating patients. When she was away at an event, sometimes for nearly two weeks in a month, that meant she was missing out on two weeks of income.

So she decided that she needed to find a better way to serve her clients without always needing to trade her time for money. That's when she committed to going all in on building an online, solutions-based moneymaker for the audience of combat athletes that she was already working with. After following the five steps, she launched her beta program with ten paying clients and 21 more on her waitlist.

Here's Robyn's story in detail: Robyn, the current owner of Move Forward Physiotherapy, started by identifying her moneymaker:

helping fighters go from broken with nagging injuries to performing their best in the ring. She realized that many fighters struggled with injuries and lacked proper guidance on recovery and performance. This was her golden opportunity.

Step 1: Planning Her Beta

Robyn laid out a clear path for her beta clients. She planned an eight-week program focusing on injury prevention, fight preparation, and peak performance. Her initial roadmap for the combat athletes that would join her beta was simple yet powerful:

- Rebuilding Training Strategies
- Master The Basics
- Avoid Injury and Optimize Performance
- Fighter Specific Strength Training
- Recover Like A Pro Without Sacrificing Training
- Head Kicks For Life - Mobility Training
- Fight Camp Changes and Weight Cuts
- Fighting Like A Pro - Next Steps

Step 2: Attracting Her Beta Clients

Knowing that a beta works best with 5-10 initial clients, Robyn created engaging content around injury prevention and performance enhancement. She posted tips, shared her own experiences, and engaged her audience with polls and questions. She then put out a call to action:

"Hey fighters, if I created an online program for fighters to go from nagging injuries to performing their best in the ring, would you be interested?" Then she linked a poll below with two options: 1. ["Heck yes - send me details!"] and 2. ["Possibly...send me the details!"].

75% of those who saw the poll and voted chose option 1, with the other 25% choosing option 2.

Step 3: Creating Hype

Robyn built anticipation through multiple posts and stories. She kept reminding her audience about the limited spots and created a sense of urgency. She shared:

"I posted 2 days ago that I'm looking for 5-10 people to join the beta launch of my online program. There have been 20 people that messaged me! 8 people have officially signed up! There are 2 spots left...so if you're interested but haven't confirmed with me...let me know asap!"

Which was followed by *"and if this beta launch isn't for you... that's ok! I have a waitlist of 7 people for the next launch already started...so I can add you to the list!"*

Step 4: Engaging in Conversations

Robyn reached out to everyone who responded to her posts. Here's how she did it: Robyn's DM Script: *"Hey [name], I wanted to personally invite you to join my beta launch of the new on-*

line program "The Fighter's Edge." It's my first time doing this program, so I'm only accepting 5-10 people to make sure you're served the best and I get feedback to make it better. Throughout the 8 weeks I will be asking for feedback to make this a really, really good program. In a private community I will also be doing live trainings based on questions, Q&A sessions, bringing in some guest speakers, doing case studies, and some other surprises."

"For the 10 people that join, the cost is $97 which is a fraction of what it will be moving forward. In the future, this program will be a monthly membership, as part of the beta group, you will receive a lifetime membership, as well as a full-blown Fighters Edge Resource Library."

"I am looking to fill these 10 spots over the course of the next couple days and I already have 7 people interested, so let me know asap. Thank you!"

Step 5: Offering Her Beta

Robyn presented her offer clearly, highlighting the benefits and the exclusive feedback opportunity. She made it easy for her clients to understand the value they were getting.

Step 6: Delivering and Improving

Robyn delivered her beta program live, gathered feedback, and made necessary adjustments. She used the feedback to refine her offer, ensuring it met the needs of her clients.

Robyn's journey is a testament to the power of a well-executed beta offer. She not only validated her moneymaker but also gained confidence and proof of her solution's value. Today, she runs a $1,200 premium program successfully. As Robyn puts it, "The beta process was a game-changer. It gave me the feedback and confidence I needed to refine my program and charge what it's truly worth."

Addressing Potential Challenges

The first challenge is simply getting comfortable with the idea of charging, which we just covered in this chapter. The second challenge is now charging what your program is worth, or charging premium prices, which we will uncover together in Chapter 6. Many people feel unsure about the value of their moneymaker, the value of their solution, or even fear rejection. One of the cheat codes is this beta process because the beta process helps you refine your solution, get real feedback, get proof, get testimonials from people, and then by default build confidence through all of that so that by the time you release it and you are able to do what I'm going to help you uncover or unlock in Chapter 6, which is now charge a premium, you're able to do it with confidence and without having to wait 10 plus years.

Trust the Process

Stay committed to this journey. You're capable of achieving more than you've ever imagined. The beta process is just the beginning. Get ready for Chapter 6, where we'll dive deep into transforming your beta into a premium offer. We'll explore the psychology behind premium pricing and how to confidently present your highest-value offer. This is where your ability to impact more people and generate more income truly begins.

NOTES

NOTES

NOTES

NOTES

CHAPTER 6

Elevate To Premium

Chapter 6

Elevate to Premium

Mastering the Transition from Beta to High-Value Offers

Embracing the Power of Premium

Imagine transforming your moneymaker and life with the power of premium pricing. Ready to uncover the secret? Welcome to the next level of your moneymaker journey. In this chapter, we're going to explore the concept of premium pricing and why it's essential for your business and your clients. We'll break down the barriers around premium pricing and show you how to transition from beta to a premium offer confidently.

Why Premium Matters

Many of us struggle with the idea of charging higher prices, often because we don't feel worthy or fear rejection. But here's the truth: the amount you charge has nothing to do with your worthiness and everything to do with the problems you solve. Charging a premium is about the value you provide and the transformation you create.

"Price is what you pay. Value is what you get." — Warren Buffett

$70 - $7,500: With our very first moneymaker, I initially wanted to charge $70 for it. I remember sitting in my small, cramped apartment, staring at my computer screen and feeling a mix of excitement and fear. I knew the product was good, but $70 seemed like a safe bet. Fast forward to today, that same offer and product is priced at $7,500. Why such a drastic change? Initially, I thought pricing was about me feeling confident or worthy. But as I unlocked what you're about to discover in this book, I realized it was about the value I provided and the problems I solved. Today, our most expensive service is $30,000 (who knows, by the time you're reading this, we might have offers that are far more expensive than even that) because the solution we provide is worth far more than that to our clients.

Think about it: What would you pay to have your biggest problem solved, or to receive guidance and direction that could potentially transform your life? This chapter is not only crucial for you but has been a game-changer for me personally, making it possible for us to impact many people.

For Example:

Imagine you're a personal trainer who has developed a unique program that guarantees clients will lose 20 pounds in 3 months while improving their overall health. Picture Sarah, a 35-year-old mother of two, who had tried every diet and fitness plan under the sun. She felt defeated and hopeless, but when she signed up for your program, everything changed. She not only lost the weight but gained confidence and energy she hadn't felt in years. People will pay a premium for that program because it solves a significant problem and transforms their lives. Your moneymaker is similar – it's about solving significant problems and creating substantial value.

The Money Math

Let's do the money math. How would you love to make an additional $2,500 a month, $5,000 a month, or even $10,000 a month within the next 6 to 12 months? Would that be something you'd be interested in? For the sake of this example, let's use $5,000.

Imagine the freedom and possibilities an extra $5,000 a month could bring. Most of us struggle with the idea because our brains default to time-for-money thinking. You might be wondering, "How would I make $5,000 more at my job?" If you're earning $20 an hour or $25 an hour, even $30 an hour, you're probably calculating the hours and thinking, "Whoa, making an extra $5,000 a month seems impossible."

But what if I told you that achieving this through solutions-for-money, not time-for-money, is not only possible but within your reach?

Here's the breakdown: $5,000 is simply 20 people paying you $250 each. Now, let's pause and reflect. Do you believe that with the right guidance and frameworks, once you've locked in your moneymaker and turned it into a beta, you can find 20 people in the entire online world who would benefit from your solution? Do you believe there are 20 people who would pay for the solution you provide? The answer should be a resounding yes.

If the answer is no, it's either your insecurity talking or you're not solving a problem that people want solved. But if it's yes—and it should be—then let's continue.

So, 20 people at $250 each. Now, let's deepen this. What if those same people want that problem solved consistently and are willing to pay you $250 every single month? That's $5,000 a month, or $60,000 a year. Just imagine the impact that could have on your life.

Let's stretch it further: What if you had 10 people paying you $500 each, or 5 people paying $1,000 each? Suddenly, $5,000 a month becomes a reachable goal, and $20,000 a month starts to feel attainable.

You might think $1,000 is a lot, but consider this: are you focusing on the price tag or the value of the solution you provide? Think about what it's already costing your clients not to solve their problems. For example, with our first moneymaker, Pre-PT Grind, we help students get into grad school, specifically physical therapy school, without wasting time or money.

Imagine a student who's been rejected from PT schools four years in a row. Every year they don't get in, they lose a year of potential income as a physical therapist. If a new grad PT makes $80,000 annually, that's $320,000 lost over four years. Picture this student, feeling the weight of another rejection letter, seeing their dreams slip further away each year. Paying us $5,000 or even $10,000 to avoid another year of rejection makes perfect sense.

We understand the true cost of not solving a problem, and that's why people are willing to pay a premium. Now, consider the power of premium pricing for your moneymaker. Could you find 20 people willing to pay $1,000 each for a solution that could transform their lives? That's $20,000 a month. This is how others are achieving exponential income growth. Many of our six-figure Mastermind clients have used these principles to dramatically increase their income while providing immense value to their clients.

Discover Your Unique Value

Identify Your Unique Value:

- List 3 to 5 unique aspects of your moneymaker that differentiate it from others.
- Reflect on how these unique aspects create value and solve significant problems for your clients.

Client Transformation Stories:

- Write down at least two client transformation stories from some of your beta clients that highlight the impact of your moneymaker.

- Reflect on these stories and identify common themes of value and transformation.

Reflection Questions:

- What specific problems does my moneymaker solve?
- How does the transformation my clients experience justify a premium price?
- In what ways can I enhance the value of my offer to further justify premium pricing?

The Cost of Not Taking Action

The two most expensive things in the world are taxes and the cost of not knowing how to solve the biggest problems in life. Think about it. The gap between where you are and where you want to be is often filled with missed opportunities and uncalculated losses.

When people don't solve their critical problems, they incur significant costs—financially and emotionally. For instance, failing to get into a desired program, missing out on career opportunities, or not achieving personal health goals can be immensely costly. Every year that passes without solving these issues can add up to a staggering amount.

Understanding this dynamic shifts the perspective on pricing. It's not about how much you're charging; it's about the value and the relief you're providing. This realization is pivotal in crafting and pricing your premium offer.

"Your price is a reflection of your self-worth. If you don't value yourself, no one else will."
— Dan Lok

Price Setting

Assessing Value The first step in pricing your premium offer is understanding the value you provide. Look at the transformation you're offering and the significant problems you're solving. Remember, people pay to move towards pleasure or away from pain.

Research and Benchmarking Research what others in your industry are charging for similar transformations. This will give you a ballpark figure. Don't be afraid to price higher if your offer provides more value.

Outcome-Based Pricing Price your services based on the outcome and transformation you provide, not the time you spend. This shifts the focus from you to the client's results, making it easier to justify higher prices.

Craft Your Premium Pricing Strategy

Research and Benchmarking:

- Research at least 3 competitors in your industry who offer similar transformations. Note their pricing strategies.
- Reflect on how your moneymaker compares in terms of value and outcomes.

Set Your Premium Price:

- Based on your value assessment and research, set a premium price for your moneymaker.
- Consider different pricing tiers (e.g., basic, standard, premium) and what additional value each tier offers.

Reflection Questions:

- What price point do I feel confident in charging, and why?
- How does my pricing compare to my competitors, and what justifies any differences?
- What additional value can I provide to support my premium pricing?

Building Your Premium Offer

When crafting your premium offer, there are four key elements that we have found to work brilliantly. In fact, in all of our premium services ranging from $3,500 to $30,000 plus, we always use these four pillars as the way in which we package our programs:

1. **Guidance:** Provide expert advice and direction.
2. **Tools:** Offer resources that help your clients implement what they've learned.
3. **Community:** Build a supportive group where clients can share experiences and learn from each other.
4. **Accountability:** Regular check-ins to ensure clients stay on track.

Having all four elements in place makes your offer more valuable and desirable.

Design Your Premium Offer

Define the Four Pillars:

- Outline how you will incorporate guidance, tools, community, and accountability into your premium offer.
- Create a detailed description of each pillar and its benefits to your clients.

Reflection Questions:

- How can I clearly communicate the benefits of each pillar in my offer?

- What testimonials or stories best illustrate the value of my offer?

Crafting Your Premium Offer

Step-by-Step Guide:

1. **Define Your Offer:** Clearly outline what your premium offer includes. Focus on outcomes and benefits.
2. **Set Your Price:** Based on your research and the value you provide, set a price that reflects the transformation you offer.
3. **Leverage Testimonials:** Use feedback from your beta clients to build credibility and demonstrate the effectiveness of your offer.
4. **Practice Your Pitch:** Rehearse your sales call framework and be prepared to address common objections.

Alex Hormozi's Value Equation

To increase the perceived value of your offer, keep in mind Alex Hormozi's value equation. There are four main components:

1. **Increased Dream Outcome:** People need to see a heightened awareness of their desired result.

2. **Increased Likelihood of Achievement:** Clients need to feel that achieving their goal is possible. Testimonials and proof from your beta clients can help here.

3. **Reduced Effort and Sacrifice:** Make your solution feel easier and less daunting than doing it alone.

4. **Reduced Time Delay:** Show clients that working with you will get them their desired outcome faster.

Understanding and incorporating these elements will help you price your services at a premium level. It's not about your years of experience but about the outcomes you deliver. The beta phase gives you validation that your process works and the confidence to charge more.

Premium Calls

One of the fastest ways to get premium clients is to get people on a call. This could be leads from your lead magnet, people engaging with your content, or those who want more help. For example, on Instagram, we might post valuable content on stories or reels and have a call to action. People who are interested can vote on a poll, comment on a post, DM you, or opt into your email sequence. Then, you offer to get on a call with them if they truly want more help.

Sales Transfer

Sales is a transfer of trust, a transfer of clarity, a transfer of confidence, and a transfer of energy. You're literally transferring these things from yourself to the person you are selling to. If you don't have that, you can't transfer it over. It's crucial to understand this dynamic to become effective in sales.

Sales Truths

Sales is actually a misunderstood concept. When you're selling, you're transferring four specific things and receiving something in return. What most of us don't realize is that we've been selling our whole lives. When you were a kid and you wanted something, you had to sell your parents on it. When you want your friends to go somewhere for dinner instead of another place, you have to sell them on the idea. You've been doing it without realizing it.

> **"The art of selling is the art of planting in the mind of another a motive which will induce voluntary action."**
> **— Edwin Louis Cole**

The reason many people mistakenly think sales is bad is that they remember the bad experiences more vividly than the good ones. One of my coaches once shared that the best sales experiences are so seamless that we don't even realize we're being persuaded. Good sales should never feel pushy or uncomfortable; instead, they should feel natural and beneficial.

This chapter will show you how to sell in a way that never feels salesy or pushy. Even if you've never sold anything before, by following these steps, you'll achieve results that even expert sales professionals struggle to get. You'll learn how to connect with people, understand their needs, and offer solutions that genuinely help them.

Perfecting Your Sales Call

Practice Your Pitch:

- Rehearse your sales call framework, focusing on the six steps outlined in the chapter.
- Role-play with a partner or record yourself to refine your approach.

Prepare for Objections:

- List common objections you might encounter during sales calls.
- Develop clear, confident responses to each objection.

Reflection Questions:

- What are the most common objections I face, and how can I address them effectively?
- How can I improve my sales pitch to better communicate the value of my offer?
- What techniques can I use to ensure I listen more and talk less during sales calls?

Sales Call Guide: Turning Interest into Investment

Purpose of a Call

A call allows you to better understand if the person is a good fit. The goal is to assess whether they have a dream outcome you can help them achieve. People pay to move towards pleasure or to escape pain. Understanding their desired outcome and pain points is crucial.

Pre-Call Preparation:

- Be clear on the call's purpose.
- Prepare to ask questions and listen more than you speak.

Starting the Call:

- Eliminate the Fluff: Get straight to the point. Greet them warmly but get to the purpose of the call quickly.
- Set Expectations: Ask for permission to outline the call's goals. "Is it cool if we get on the same page regarding what the purpose of this call is?"

Six Sales Steps

1. **Understanding Their Why/Dream Outcome:**
   - *Question:* "Why is achieving this goal important to you?"
   - *Clarify:* Paraphrase their answer to show understanding. "So what I'm hearing is that achieving [desired outcome] is important because [reason]. Is that correct?"
2. **Exposing Their Roadblocks:**
   - *Question:* "Let's talk about where you're currently stuck. What are the biggest challenges you're facing right now in achieving this goal?"
   - *Clarify:* "So, you're struggling with [challenge]. Are there any other obstacles?"
3. **Understanding Their Current Plan:**
   - *Question:* "What have you tried so far to overcome these challenges?"
   - *Clarify:* "It sounds like you've tried [solution] and it hasn't worked as well as you'd hoped. What else have you considered?"
4. **Future-Pacing:**
   - *Question:* "Imagine for a moment that you've achieved your goal. What does that feel like? Who are you telling first?"

- *Clarify:* "So, it sounds like achieving [desired outcome] would be a huge relief and a major milestone for you. Is that right?"

5. **Providing Guidance:**
    - *Strategy:* Offer three actionable strategies tailored to their challenges.
    - *Example:* For fitness coaching, you might suggest focusing on nutrition, workout consistency, and mindset shifts.
    - *Clarify:* Ask if they have questions about the strategies you've shared.

6. **Transition to a Sale:**
    - *Question:* "Do you want my help in achieving this goal?"
    - *Clarify:* "Great! Based on our conversation, it sounds like you'd be a great fit for my program. Would you like me to share how the program works and the investment details?"

Persuasion Ninja Strategy

Now before I show you an example of a sales call done well, let's talk about a crucial mistake many people make that costs them thousands of dollars. It's talking too much on a sales call. Your prospect should be doing most of the talking. In fact, the best sales calls I've ever had involve the prospect doing close to 80% of the talking.

This might seem counterintuitive because many think the more we talk, the more value we provide. In reality, the more we talk, the less heard your prospect feels and the more overwhelmed they become. This is why many of us have had bad sales experiences where someone talks our ear off trying to convince us to do something we didn't want to do. Does this make sense?

The more you let them talk, the more they will persuade themselves. If you try to convince them, it won't work. But if you ask enough questions, they will do all the persuading for you if they are the right fit. They will do most of the work for you if you just listen.

If you're a terrible listener, you will struggle with sales. But if you are a brilliant listener, don't be surprised when people want to pay you thousands of dollars over time. One of the best ways to do this is to clarify whenever you get an answer. Instead of rambling off tips and strategies, refrain from that and clarify. The best way to clarify is by asking a question or paraphrasing what they said.

For example, if they tell you their biggest obstacles, don't just say, "Oh, I see that all the time. Our clients experience that." Instead, say, "So what I'm hearing you say is," and restate what they just said. Then, if you have a clarifying question, ask, "If you don't mind my asking, what is it about [said problem] that has made it so difficult for you?" You're digging deeper with curiosity.

Curiosity is a cheat code. When you approach a sales conversation with a curious tone, more interested in them and helping them than in getting them to buy, that's very powerful.

Lastly, think of it like a game of tag. If you come to a sales call with "sales breath," it feels like you need them to buy, which will make them run away. But if you're neutral, present, and curious, they will feel like they need you more than you need them. This is when they become more attracted to your opportunity.

Call Example

Introduction: "Hey, how are you doing? Looking forward to learning more about you today and seeing if there's any way I can assist you in your journey. Are you ready to begin?"

Set Expectations: "Before we dive in, is it cool if we get on the same page regarding the purpose of this call? The biggest goal of this call is to see if we're a good fit to work together. I want to understand your situation better and, if there's a fit, share how I can potentially help. Does that sound good?"

Step 1: Understanding Their Why/Dream Outcome: "Great! So, before we talk about where you're stuck, can you share why achieving this goal is so important to you?" *Clarify:* "So what I'm hearing is that achieving [desired outcome] is important because [reason]. Is that correct?"

Step 2: Exposing Their Roadblocks: "Let's talk about where you're currently stuck. What are the biggest challenges you're facing right now in achieving this goal?" *Clarify:* "So, you're struggling with [challenge]. Are there any other obstacles?"

Step 3: Understanding Their Current Plan: "Can you tell me what you've tried so far to overcome these challenges?"*Clarify:* "It sounds like you've tried [solution] and it hasn't worked as well as you'd hoped. What else have you considered?"

Step 4: Future-Pacing: "Imagine for a moment that you've achieved your goal. What does that feel like? Who are you telling first?" *Clarify:* "So, it sounds like achieving [desired outcome] would be a huge relief and a major milestone for you. Is that right?"

Step 5: Providing Guidance: "Based on what you've shared, here are three strategies that I think could really help you move forward:

1. Nutrition: Tailoring your diet to support your fitness goals.

2. Workout Consistency: Creating a sustainable workout plan.

3. Mindset Shifts: Developing a positive and resilient mindset."

"Do you have any questions about these strategies?" *Clarify:* Answer any questions they have and ensure they understand the suggestions.

Step 6: Transition to a Sale: "Do you want my help in achieving this goal?" *Clarify:* "Great! Based on our conversation, it sounds like you'd be a great fit for my program. Would you like me to share how the program works and the investment details?"

Presenting the Offer

When you present your offer, focus on the payoff rather than detailing every feature. People don't buy the parts; they buy the outcome. Here's how to present your premium program effectively:

Highlight the Payoff:

- Emphasize the results your clients will achieve. Explain the benefits of your guidance, tools, accountability, and community.
- **Guidance:** "With my personalized coaching, you'll gain the clarity and direction needed to achieve your goals faster."
- **Tools:** "The resources I provide will simplify the process, making implementation straightforward and effective."
- **Accountability:** "Regular check-ins ensure you stay on track and motivated, increasing your chances of success."
- **Community:** "You'll join a supportive network of like-minded individuals, fostering growth and shared learning."

Communicate Value: Make it clear how your program solves their problems and transforms their lives. "My program includes personalized coaching, detailed workout plans, and ongoing support to ensure you achieve your goals."

Discuss Investment: Be straightforward about the cost and flexible payment options. "The investment for this program is [price], and we offer flexible payment plans to make it accessible."

Address Objections: Be prepared to answer any questions or concerns they may have. "How does that sound to you? Do you have any questions about how this program can help you achieve your goals?"

Close the Call: Encourage them to take action without being pushy. "Are you ready to get started today?"

By focusing on the outcomes and benefits, you'll keep the conversation engaging and relevant, ensuring your prospect sees the value in your premium offer.

Persuasion vs. Convincing

Persuasion: Getting someone to do something for their own reasons. **Convincing:** Getting someone to do something for your reasons.

Example Questions:

- Before discussing investment: "Why do you believe this program will work for you?"
- To create urgency: "Why take action on this now and not six months from now? Why not a year from now?"

Addressing Common Fears About Premium Pricing

Common Fears: It's natural to fear rejection or feel unworthy. Remember, higher pricing attracts more committed clients.

> **"The only way to achieve the impossible is to believe it is possible."**
> **— Charles Kingsleigh**

Myron Golden's Insight: "If you're the cheapest, no one will ever believe you're the best, and if you're the best, no one will ever expect you to be the cheapest." This emphasizes the importance of pricing as a signal of value and quality.

Trust and Invest

Embrace the Journey Understand that having a coach can help you personalize and refine your approach, ensuring success. Your clients are out there, ready to pay a premium for the transformation you offer.

Implement Your Premium Pricing Strategy

Set a Premium Price for Your Moneymaker:

- Based on your value assessment and research, finalize a premium price for your moneymaker. Write it down and commit to it.

Conduct Sales Calls:

- Schedule at least three sales calls in the next week. Use the six steps of a sales call and the persuasion ninja strategies to guide your conversations.

Gather Feedback:

- After each sales call, ask for feedback from your prospects. Use this feedback to refine your pitch and approach.

Invest in Personal Development:

- Commit to ongoing personal development in sales and pricing strategies. Read books, attend workshops, and seek out mentors to continually improve your skills.

Final Thoughts

Congratulations on mastering the art of premium pricing! You've learned how to assess the true value of your moneymaker, set a price that reflects the transformation you offer, and effectively communicate that value to your clients. By implementing these strategies, you're not only increasing your income but also attracting more committed and satisfied clients.

In Chapter 7, we'll dive deeper into scaling your moneymaker through leverage, ensuring you maximize both your income and impact. Get ready to learn how to save time, impact more people, and generate more income with less effort. We'll explore the power of technology, the importance of systems, and the magic of one-to-many offers. This next chapter is going to unlock the true potential of your moneymaker. Let's get it!

NOTES

NOTES

NOTES

NOTES

CHAPTER 7

Leverage Tech And Time

Chapter 7

Leverage Tech & Time

Maximizing Impact and Income with Smart Strategies

Leverage: Your Key to Big Results

You've made it this far, and I bet you're wondering, "Can I really pull this off?" Maybe you're feeling overwhelmed, thinking you're too busy or that you don't have anyone to help you. Trust me, I get it. But here's the good news—you don't need a huge team or endless hours in a day to make this work. What you need is leverage.

> **"Leverage is the reason some people become rich and others do not become rich."**
> **— Robert Kiyosaki**

Leverage is about achieving bigger results with the same or even less effort. It's about working smarter, not harder. Think about a lever—small, strategic actions can yield significant results when you understand how to apply leverage correctly.

In this chapter, we're diving into how to:

- **Make Every Minute Count**: Manage your time effectively to maximize productivity.
- **Boost Success with Technology**: Use affordable tech tools to handle tasks that used to require a whole team.
- **Build Your Dream Team**: Understand the potential of hiring experts who excel in their roles, while focusing on technology initially to substitute for a team.
- **Skill Mastery: The Compound Effect**: Learn how improving your skills over time leads to exponential growth in your moneymaker's success.

Making Every Minute Count

Let's start with one of the most crucial elements: leveraging your time. Time management can significantly impact your journey to success, and often it's overlooked.

One of our top coaches, Alayna, recently shared valuable insights with some of our bootcamp clients about leveraging time. Her principles are incredibly relevant here. One key principle is awareness. Many people aren't fully aware of where their time goes. Doing a time audit can reveal surprising amounts of wasted time. It might seem tedious, but it's eye-opening. Track everything you do for two weeks. By writing down every task and distraction, you'll get a clear picture of how you're actually spending your time.

Conduct a Time Audit

- **Track Your Time**: For two weeks, log every activity you do each day, including how long each task takes. Be honest and detailed.
- **Identify Patterns**: Review your log to identify patterns and time wasters. Where are you losing time? What activities can you cut back on or eliminate?
- **Prioritize Tasks**: Rank your activities by importance. Focus on tasks that align with your goals and eliminate or reduce lower-priority activities.

Imagine you sleep for eight hours and work a traditional nine-to-five job. That accounts for 16 hours of your day, leaving you with eight hours of 'free' time. Many feel they have no time, but those eight hours are often unstructured and driven by emotions rather than intention. How often do you find yourself mindlessly scrolling through social media or binge-watching a show? Those activities eat up your valuable time without providing any meaningful return.

"The key is not to prioritize what's on your schedule, but to schedule your priorities." — Stephen Covey

Alayna pointed out that when we don't do what we say we will, we lose self-respect. It's about keeping promises to yourself, which builds confidence and self-esteem. Consistency is key. Motivation fluctuates because it's an emotion, but a solid time management system keeps you on track even when motivation wanes. This is crucial for your moneymaker because, without a boss to dictate your schedule, your progress relies entirely on your discipline.

Create a Time Management System

- **Set a Routine**: Develop a daily routine that includes time for your top priorities. Stick to this routine as closely as possible.
- **Use Tools**: Leverage tools like calendars, planners, and apps to schedule your tasks and set reminders.
- **Review Regularly**: Regularly review your schedule and adjust as needed to stay aligned with your goals.

Alayna's principles highlight that understanding and optimizing your time leads to greater self-respect and fulfillment. It's about creating a life where you do what you say you will, showing up for yourself and your goals consistently. This foundation of self-respect and disciplined time management will propel you forward, making all other forms of leverage more effective.

One-to-Many vs. One-on-One

Before diving into technology and people, it's crucial to understand the different types of leverage, specifically the shift from one-on-one to one-to-many interactions.

When you start, you might be engaging with clients or customers one-on-one. This is valuable but limits your reach and scalability. The real magic happens when you transition to a one-to-many model. This means creating systems, content, or services that can impact multiple people simultaneously.

Think about it: instead of coaching one person at a time, you could be hosting a free or paid 60 to 90-minute class, creating an online course, or publishing a book that helps hundreds or even thousands at once. This shift dramatically amplifies your impact without significantly increasing your effort.

When we first started, my business partner Casey and I were doing one-on-one coaching sessions. It was fulfilling but also exhausting and limited the number of people we could help because we were capped on how much time we could actually spend on it. At the time, we were either in school or working as new grad physical therapists. As our understanding of leverage grew, we shifted to creating pre-built courses and coaching programs, and teaching one-to-many instead of one-to-one. This allowed us to reach more people and generate more income with the same amount of effort.

Here's a real-life example of how powerful this can be. We often run masterclasses, and one in particular stands out in my mind. We sometimes do these masterclasses to offer free value, and then at the end of those classes, we usually give people an opportunity to work with us and join one of our programs. For one particular class, we had about 200 people sign up for the free class, and it was about 90 minutes long. Out of the 200 people, usually about 30-35% show up live to free classes, mainly because they had not invested in them, so about 60 people showed up live. Out of those 60, 23 ended up purchasing our offer.

Now, think about the time difference here. Imagine if I had had to speak to 60 people one-on-one, which, for us, a one-on-one conversation is about 45 minutes. That would have been about 2,700 minutes, or 45 hours. But by using the one-to-many masterclass approach, I was able to accomplish that in just 90 minutes and then went on to enjoy dinner with my family. Would you rather spend 45 hours or 90 minutes to get the same outcome? The answer is obvious, right?

Shift from One-to-One to One-to-Many

Reflect on your current or future moneymaker model. Are there areas where you can shift from one-on-one to one-to-many? Write down one strategy that you can implement to make this shift.

Boosting Success with Technology

Now, let's dive into how technology can transform your moneymaker. Technology is a game-changer when it comes to leveraging your efforts. We live in a time where artificial intelligence (AI) and software can handle many tasks that used to require significant human effort. Here's how you can harness these tools effectively.

Implement New Tools

- **Choose Your Tools**: Select one or two AI tools or software programs to integrate into your moneymaker operations.
- **Monitor Impact**: Use the selected tools for a month, monitoring their impact on your productivity and efficiency.
- **Evaluate Effectiveness**: After a month, evaluate how these tools have improved your ability to manage tasks and serve your clients. Make adjustments as necessary.

Artificial Intelligence (AI)

AI is transforming how moneymakers operate. Here are some ways you can leverage AI:

- **Content Creation**: AI can help generate ideas, write articles, and even create videos. Imagine having an AI tool that understands your audience and can produce high-quality content tailored to their needs.

- **Customer Interaction**: AI chatbots can handle customer inquiries, book appointments, and even close sales. This means you can provide excellent customer service without being available 24/7.
- **Data Analysis**: AI can analyze large sets of data to provide insights into your audience's behavior, preferences, and trends. This allows you to make informed decisions and tailor your offerings to meet their needs precisely.

Software Tools

Beyond AI, there are numerous software tools that can automate and streamline your moneymaker operations:

- **Email Marketing**: Tools like Mailchimp and ConvertKit automate your email campaigns, ensuring your audience receives timely and relevant content.
- **Customer Relationship Management (CRM)**: Systems like HubSpot, Salesforce, and Go High Level help you manage and analyze customer interactions and data throughout the customer lifecycle, improving business relationships.
- **Project Management**: Tools like Trello and Asana help you keep track of tasks, deadlines, and collaborate with your team efficiently.

For our coaching clients, we provide them with a pre-built comprehensive software that hosts everything they need: emails, conversations, websites, landing pages, and automations for lead magnets. This integration makes their moneymaker operations smooth and efficient, allowing them to focus on what they do best—serving their clients. This seamless integration is a key feature we emphasize in our Impact to Income University Coaching Program, helping our clients maximize their efficiency and impact.

The key to leveraging technology is to integrate it seamlessly into your operations so that it enhances your efficiency and productivity without overwhelming you. Start with one or two tools, master them, and then gradually incorporate more as you grow.

Technology as Your Initial Team

- **Use Technology to Handle Tasks**: Use technology to handle tasks that a team would typically manage. Identify key areas where technology can be most effective.
- **Reflection Question**: How has leveraging technology allowed you to operate more efficiently without a large team?

Building Your Dream Team

Let's talk about leveraging people. Hiring experts who excel in their roles can take your moneymaker to new heights. Today, in our moneymakers, we have experts in key positions who are outstanding at what they do. In fact, they're often better than me at those roles, which makes our operations much more efficient and allows us to serve more people at a higher level.

There's a beautiful time and place for hiring a team. However, the mistake people make when starting this journey is thinking that they need to wait until they can afford a team, which means they likely never start. They believe they need to build their moneymaker to afford the team they think they need, which is backwards. That's why leveraging technology becomes the initial step.

Eventually, as you grow, you'll want to communicate with your clients, have sales calls handled for you, and ensure your clients are taken care of and guided effectively. At this stage, hiring people who are really good at what they do becomes crucial. This is what we've done, and it's allowed us to reach new heights.

Right now, you might not be at this stage yet, but it's important to know that this is coming down the line for you. Knowing this can help you plan and stay motivated. For now, leverage technology to mimic what a team would do, giving you the foundation you need to grow.

Skill Mastery: The Compound Effect

Now, let's talk about how your moneymaker compounds over time. At a job, getting better might mean a small raise. With your moneymaker, getting better means making exponentially more money. Let's break this down with more depth and practical insight.

Track Your Progress

- **Set Clear Goals**: Define your income and impact goals for the next year, three years, and five years.
- **Track Your Efforts**: Keep a journal of your activities, noting what works and what doesn't.
- **Review and Reflect**: Regularly review your progress. Celebrate your successes and learn from your failures.

The 'Income' Compound Effect

When you start your moneymaker journey, it might feel like an uphill battle. You're learning new things, adapting to new challenges, and pushing through obstacles. This is where the concept of the income compound effect comes into play. It's about understanding that your income grows exponentially as you get better, not linearly.

Let me share our journey to illustrate this:

In our first year, we made $1,200. It wasn't much, but we knew we were laying the foundation. We focused on getting better, understanding our audience, and refining our approach. In the second year, our income grew to $12,500. Still modest, but it was a tenfold increase from the first year.

By the third year, we made $97,000. The income growth started to reflect our increased expertise and efficiency. In the fourth year, we hit a quarter of a million dollars, and by the fifth year, we made half a million. As I write this book, we are seven plus years into being in business, and the better we get, the bigger problems we can solve, the more revenue we will continue to generate.

"Small daily improvements over time lead to stunning results."
— Robin Sharma

It's important to understand that sometimes it may take you longer than someone else, and that's okay. Don't compare your journey to others. This is where we often get tripped up—seeing people on Instagram with super nice cars and thinking, "They're making a lot of money; I should be able to make money super fast." Everyone's path is different.

What if we had quit after year one? Or year two? You wouldn't be reading this book. We wouldn't be living the life we live today, helping the clients we help today, transforming the lives we're able to touch today. The people who don't honor the income compound effect, who don't understand that the better they get, the more they'll be paid—unlike any job—are the ones who quit too early and will never be successful. If that's what you decide to do, maybe this book isn't for you. But if you're willing to outlast the learning curve, to go from being really bad to becoming really good by putting in the repetitions and letting everything fall into place as it should, then you will absolutely dominate.

Moving Forward with Leverage

As you prepare for the next chapter, remember that impact is the goal, and income simply follows. We're going to put all the pieces together in Chapter 8, setting you up to take massive action and transform not only your life but also the lives of those you will impact.

Incorporate these principles, apply the practical exercises, and watch how leverage transforms your moneymaker into a powerful force for good. The journey may start uphill, but with the right leverage, you'll soon find yourself coasting downhill with momentum on your side.

Stay committed, keep pushing forward, and remember: the better you get, the more people you can help, and the more your income will grow.

NOTES

NOTES

NOTES

NOTES

CHAPTER 8

Build Your Legacy

Chapter 8

Building Your Legacy

Creating Lasting Impact and Financial Freedom

Transforming Your Potential

By now, you should truly see and believe that it's possible for you to impact more people and generate more income, starting now. By executing everything we've discussed and everything you'll continue to unlock in this chapter, you can achieve these goals. This journey isn't just about creating a moneymaker; it's about transforming your life and the lives of those you will impact. Becoming an entrepreneur is both challenging and immensely rewarding.

Embracing Your New Identity

Without even realizing it, you've already stepped into the shoes of an entrepreneur. This term often conjures images of big-time business moguls, but it's much simpler and more profound. You are now an entrepreneur because you've taken the leap to create something valuable, solve problems, and make an impact.

Imagine this journey as climbing a mountain. Each step might be tough, the path might be steep, but the view from the top is worth every effort. You are now on that path, and with every step, you are becoming stronger and more capable.

Reflect: How has your perception of being an entrepreneur changed since you started reading this book?

Disruption Always Follows Intention

Have you ever wondered why every time you aim to upgrade your life, obstacles seem to appear almost instantly? Whether it's joining a program to build your moneymaker or setting a new goal, internal and external battles arise. What I'm about to share changed the game for me, and it can change it for you too.

Myron Golden's Insight: If you want to be successful, remember that disruption always follows intention. This means anytime you want to upgrade your life—be it finances, fitness, or faith—there will be something trying to hold you back. But once you learn to ignore these disruptions and push forward, you become unstoppable.

Think of it like planting a garden. When you plant a seed, weeds inevitably try to choke it. But if you keep tending to your garden, pulling out the weeds, and nurturing your plants, you'll eventually see them grow strong and bear fruit.

Disruption Diary

- **Keep a Journal for a Week:** Each day, write down any disruptions or obstacles you face as you work towards your goals.
- **Note How You Responded:** Note how you responded to each disruption and what you learned from it.
- **Reflect:** Think about a recent disruption you faced. How did it test your commitment to your goals?

The Weight of Being the "One"

Being the "one" in your family or circle who decides to break the mold is a heavy responsibility. Ed Mylett often discusses the unique burden and privilege of being a trailblazer. The one who steps out, takes risks, and pursues a different path carries the hopes and dreams of those who came before and those who will follow.

Howard Schultz's Journey: Schultz grew up in a poor family, working hard to change his circumstances. He saw an opportunity with a small coffee shop named Starbucks and transformed it into a global brand. His journey wasn't easy; he faced numerous rejections and financial struggles. Yet, he persevered, carrying the weight of being the one who would change his family's legacy forever.

"Dream big dreams. Only big dreams have the power to move men's souls."
— Marcus Aurelius

Overcoming Obstacles

Every entrepreneur faces roadblocks. It's not about avoiding them but learning how to navigate through them. The journey of being an entrepreneur is filled with highs and lows. The key is to keep moving forward, even when things seem tough.

Jeff Bezos' Perspective: Bezos famously said, "I knew that if I failed, I wouldn't regret that, but I knew the one thing I might regret is not trying." He faced numerous challenges in building Amazon, from financial difficulties to intense competition. But he saw every challenge as an opportunity, which allowed him to build one of the most successful companies in the world.

Failure Reflection

- **Reflect on Past Failures:** Write about a past failure and how it set you up for later success.
- **Identify the Lessons Learned:** Identify the lessons learned and how they can be applied to your current goals.
- **Reflect:** What is one roadblock you are currently facing? How can you reframe it as an opportunity?

Sarah Blakely's Determination: Blakely, the founder of Spanx, faced rejection from countless investors. She started her business with $5,000 and a clear vision. Despite the setbacks, she remained determined. Today, Spanx is a billion-dollar company, and Blakely is a self-made billionaire.

"It's important to be willing to make mistakes. The worst thing that can happen is you become memorable."
— Sarah Blakely

Oprah Winfrey's Resilience: Oprah faced numerous personal and professional challenges. From a troubled childhood to career setbacks, she never let obstacles deter her. Her resilience and ability to turn challenges into opportunities made her one of the most influential figures in the world.

Henry Ford's Innovation: Ford faced bankruptcy and numerous failures before revolutionizing the automobile industry with the Model T. His ability to see beyond immediate failures and focus on long-term goals set him apart.

"Failure is simply the opportunity to begin again, this time more intelligently."
— Henry Ford

Walt Disney's Vision: Disney faced numerous setbacks, including being fired from a newspaper job for "lacking imagination." His vision and creativity eventually led to the creation of one of the most beloved entertainment companies in the world.

Support Network

Surrounding yourself with the right people is crucial. Sometimes, this means being part of virtual communities or mastermind groups where you can connect with like-minded individuals. A powerful example of this is the story of Briana Drapp, one of our six-figure mastermind coaching clients.

As I write this book, Briana is currently in her last year of physical therapy school. By the time you read this, she'll likely be a doctor of physical therapy. She's also a licensed physical therapist assistant. About two years ago, before she even got into PT school, she started working with Casey and myself. At that time, she didn't know exactly where she was headed, but she knew she wanted more from her life than just going to a clinic every day.

During one of her clinical rotations, she encountered a physical therapist who constantly complained about being overwhelmed with debt and feeling burnt out. This PT's negativity and dissatisfaction struck a chord with Briana. She knew she didn't want to become that cynical, burnt-out professional. Her goal was always to ensure she would still love what she was doing five years down the line.

Realizing the need to secure her financial future, Briana decided she had to find a way to generate additional income while still in school. She started working with Casey and myself to build something beyond the traditional clinical path. That's how she created PTA Elevation, a platform dedicated to helping physical therapist assistant students pass the national physical therapy examination.

Throughout this year, Briana has been averaging between $15,000 and $31,800 a month from her moneymaker. Her success is a testament to the power of having the right people in your corner. Briana's journey shows that you can avoid becoming disillusioned and trapped in a career you don't love by choosing to surround yourself with supportive, innovative, and like-minded individuals.

Briana often shares her experiences and insights with our community. She says, "Casey and Joses are going to teach you the things that I saw on that first day where I decided that I needed to change something. And I needed to realize it was possible.

You are 100 percent in control of your life. Being that cynical PT buried in hundreds of thousands of dollars in debt does not have to be your end goal. This is something that's definitely possible for all of you guys. Just realize that all you have to do is open your mind to the possibilities that can happen once you realize you want to choose yourself and your own future."

Briana's story exemplifies how the right mentorship and community can unlock new capabilities within yourself that you didn't even know you had. Her success story reflects the profound impact our Six-Figure Mastermind program can have, providing the essential mentorship and community support needed to achieve remarkable success. With the right people around you, you can achieve more than you ever imagined. Briana is currently generating more income while still in school than 99% of people in the physical therapy profession, which is truly mind-blowing.

Identify Your Inner Circle

- **List the Five People:** Write down the five people you spend the most time with.
- **Reflect on Their Influence:** Reflect on how each person influences your mindset and goals.
- **Reflect:** Who are the five people you spend the most time with, and how do they influence your mindset and goals?

Create Impact and Build a Legacy

Building a legacy is about more than just financial success. It's about the long-term impact you leave on the world. This involves having a clear vision and giving back to your community.

Long-term Vision: What do you want to be remembered for? How do you want to impact future generations? Having a long-term vision helps you stay focused on your goals, even when challenges arise.

Legacy Definition

- **Define Your Legacy in 7 Days:** Spend 30 minutes each day for the next week reflecting on what you want your legacy to be.

Success Visualization

- **Visualize Your Success:** Spend 10 minutes each day visualizing yourself achieving your goals. Imagine the impact on your life and the lives of others.
- **Reflect:** How does this visualization motivate you to keep pushing forward?

Believe in Your Unique Potential

Remember, you have unique gifts and strengths that no one else has. Believe in your potential to solve problems and create value. This journey is about unlocking what's already inside you. Trust the process and stay committed. You are capable of achieving more than you ever imagined.

Your Journey Begins Now

As you continue this journey, remember that you are now an entrepreneur. Embrace this new identity with all its challenges and rewards. The path may not be easy, but it is incredibly fulfilling. Stay focused, keep pushing forward, and never forget the impact you can have on the world. Your journey is just beginning, and the legacy you build will be a testament to your perseverance and dedication.

> **"The best way to predict the future is to create it."**
> **— Peter Drucker**

NOTES

NOTES

NOTES

NOTES

BONUS CHAPTER

Embracing AI:
The Ultimate Cheat Code

Bonus Chapter

Embracing AI - Your Secret Weapon for Success

I hope by now you're starting to see and believe that it's possible for you to impact more people and generate more income starting now. As we wrap up this journey, I want to give you a powerful bonus chapter on a topic that's reshaping our world: Artificial Intelligence (AI).

Many of us have heard the buzz about AI, and with it comes a mix of excitement and fear. The media often paints a picture of AI taking over jobs, creating a future where machines replace humans. But let's dive deeper and dispel some of these myths, shifting our perspective to see AI not as a threat but as a powerful ally.

The AI Fear Factor

It's natural to fear what we don't understand. The idea of machines taking over jobs can be daunting. However, it's essential to recognize that while AI will indeed change the job landscape, it's not about replacing people but augmenting our capabilities. AI is designed to handle repetitive tasks, allowing us to focus on what truly matters – creativity, strategy, and human connection.

Think about how much of your daily work involves routine, repetitive tasks. Imagine freeing up that time to focus on higher-level activities that can drive your moneymaker forward. That's the real promise of AI – enhancing our abilities and allowing us to achieve more with less effort.

The Shift Already Happening

AI is already transforming industries. From healthcare to finance, marketing to customer service, businesses that leverage AI are seeing significant benefits. Here are a few examples:

- **Healthcare:** AI assists doctors in diagnosing diseases faster and more accurately. It analyzes vast amounts of data to provide insights that would take humans much longer to uncover.
- **Finance:** AI algorithms predict market trends, helping investors make smarter decisions. Automated trading systems outperform human traders by processing data in real-time.
- **Marketing:** Personalized marketing campaigns driven by AI increase customer engagement and conversion rates. AI analyzes consumer behavior to tailor messages that resonate on a personal level.

These examples show that AI is not just a futuristic concept; it's a present reality that's enhancing our abilities and driving success.

Leveraging AI to Build Your Moneymaker

Now, let's bring this closer to home. How can you, as a moneymaker, leverage AI to build your income streams and create impact?

- **Automate Repetitive Tasks:** Use AI tools to handle routine tasks like scheduling, data entry, and customer inquiries. This frees up your time to focus on strategic growth activities.
- **Enhance Customer Experience:** AI-powered chatbots provide instant customer support, improving satisfaction and retention. Personalized recommendations based on AI analysis boost sales and engagement.
- **Data-Driven Decisions:** AI can analyze vast amounts of data to uncover trends and insights. Use these insights to make informed decisions about your business strategy, marketing efforts, and product development.

The Winners Are the Early Adopters

History has shown that those who embrace new technologies early are often the ones who win big. Look at the rise of the internet, social media, and smartphones. The pioneers who saw the potential and leveraged these tools early on are now industry leaders. The same opportunity exists with AI.

By embracing AI now, you're positioning yourself ahead of the curve. You're not just keeping up with the competition; you're setting the pace. The key is to see AI as a tool that works for you, not against you.

Dispelling the Myths

Let's address some common myths about AI:

- **AI Will Take All Our Jobs:** While AI will change the nature of work, it will also create new job opportunities. The key is to adapt and learn how to work alongside AI.
- **AI Is Too Complex:** Many AI tools are designed to be user-friendly. You don't need to be a tech expert to use them. Start with simple applications and gradually explore more advanced tools.
- **AI Is Only for Big Companies:** AI is becoming increasingly accessible to small and medium-sized businesses. There are affordable AI solutions tailored for different business needs.

Your Action Plan

To leverage AI effectively, start with these steps:

- **Educate Yourself:** Stay informed about AI trends and tools relevant to your industry. Follow thought leaders and attend webinars or workshops.

- **Experiment:** Start small by integrating AI tools into your business processes. Monitor the results and adjust as needed.
- **Collaborate:** Join communities of AI enthusiasts and entrepreneurs. Share experiences and learn from others who are on the same journey.

By taking these steps, you'll be well on your way to harnessing the power of AI and transforming your moneymaker.

Embrace the Future

AI is not just a trend; it's the future of business. By embracing it now, you're setting yourself up for success. Remember, the goal is not to fear AI but to leverage it to achieve your dreams. You're equipped with the tools and mindset needed to thrive in this new era.

As you continue your journey, keep an open mind and be ready to adapt. The future is bright for those who are willing to innovate and embrace new possibilities. AI is here to help you unlock your hidden income, impact more lives, and create the financial freedom you desire.

Wake Up to the Opportunity

If you sleep on this, you'll miss a massive opportunity. AI is rapidly advancing and those who ignore it will be left behind. The world is changing, and AI is at the forefront of that change. Embrace it, learn it, and let it propel you to new heights. The tools are in your hands, the knowledge is at your fingertips. It's up to you to take action and seize the opportunity.

Your Next Steps

1. **Stay Informed:** Subscribe to AI newsletters, follow thought leaders on social media, and join AI-focused communities.

2. **Experiment with AI Tools:** Start integrating AI into your daily tasks and business operations. Use tools like chatbots, data analysis software, and automation platforms.

3. **Collaborate and Learn:** Join workshops, attend seminars, and collaborate with AI enthusiasts. Sharing knowledge and experiences will accelerate your learning curve.

Final Thoughts

AI is not here to replace you; it's here to empower you. Embrace it, leverage it, and let it be the catalyst that drives your success. The future is yours to shape. Step into this new frontier with confidence and excitement. You have everything you need to thrive in this AI-driven world. Go out there and make your mark.

So, let's step into this new frontier together and make the most of the incredible opportunities that AI has to offer.

NOTES

NOTES

NOTES

NOTES

YOUR NEXT MOVE

Your Next Move

As we reach the final pages of this book, I invite you to pause and reflect. Remember the moment you picked up this book—filled with curiosity, perhaps a touch of skepticism, and a flicker of hope. You sought a way out of the relentless cycle of debt, financial stress, and uncertainty. You wondered if true financial freedom and peace of mind were within your reach.

Now, you stand at a pivotal moment, equipped with powerful knowledge, transformative strategies, and a renewed sense of purpose. You've dismantled the myths that once held you captive—the falsehoods that told you financial success was reserved for a select few or that hard work alone was the key to prosperity. You've discovered a more profound truth: real wealth and freedom are born from working smart, leveraging your unique gifts, and creating genuine value in ways that resonate deeply with your soul.

The Transformative Power of Mindset

One of the most significant shifts you've made on this journey is in your mindset. You've challenged and reshaped your core beliefs about money, understanding that the narratives you've held onto since childhood need not dictate your financial future. You've seen through the experiences of others—like Ashley, Joel, and Briana—that altering your money beliefs is not just a possibility; it's a necessity. This transformation is your foundation, your new truth, and it empowers you to build a life of abundance and purpose.

Reflect: How has your perception of being an entrepreneur changed since you started reading this book?

Remember when Ashley shared her story? She stood on the brink of giving up, her dreams nearly crushed by the weight of financial stress. Yet, by shifting her beliefs and embracing her unique path, she found a way to turn her passion into a thriving venture. Her journey, much like your own, is a testament to the incredible power of a transformed mindset.

Discovering Your Unique Path

You've uncovered your unique moneymaker—the distinctive blend of skills, passions, and talents that sets you apart. Whether you're drawn to teaching, coaching, creating, or innovating, you've realized that you have something extraordinarily valuable to offer the world. You understand now that the bigger the problem you solve, the greater the rewards. Through leveraging technology, community, and smart strategies, you've learned that you can magnify your impact and income exponentially.

Reflect: What unique skills and passions have you discovered during this journey?

Picture Joel, who once believed that traditional hard work was his only path to success. By embracing his natural talents and recognizing the value he could provide, he transformed his career and his life. His journey from doubt to confidence mirrors the potential within you to discover and develop your unique gifts.

Building Your Legacy

This journey isn't merely about accruing wealth; it's about crafting a legacy. It's about the enduring impact you will leave—not just for yourself, but for your family, your community, and the world at large. You've envisioned your future, identified the obstacles in your path, and committed to actionable steps that will turn your dreams into reality. You've come to understand that building a legacy transcends financial success; it's about the meaningful change you instill in the world.

Reflect: What legacy do you want to create for your family and community?

Reflect on Briana's story, where she leveraged her expertise to create a business that not only provided for her family but also empowered her community. Her legacy is one of impact and transformation, a beacon of what's possible when you align your work with your values.

Stepping Into Your Power

As you move forward, hold these truths close:

- **Embrace Your Potential:** Trust in your unique gifts and strengths. Embrace the journey of becoming a beacon of change, with all its trials and triumphs.
- **Harness Smart Strategies:** Leverage every tool at your disposal to maximize your time and impact. Use technology, build systems, and foster communities to achieve more than you ever thought possible.
- **Commit Relentlessly:** The path to true success is neither easy nor straight, but it is incredibly rewarding. Stay resolute in your goals, continue to push forward, and always remember the profound impact you are capable of creating.

Joses Final Thoughts

Before you close this chapter of our journey together, take a moment to truly absorb what you've learned and how you've transformed. Reflect on the beliefs you've shattered, the skills you've unearthed, and the vision you've crafted for your future. This is not an end, but a beginning. Your journey to financial freedom and lasting impact is just commencing.

Picture yourself standing at the edge of a vast, open field. The horizon stretches out before you, filled with endless possibilities. This is your moment to step forward, to embrace the future you've envisioned with confidence and determination.

Reflect: How does this visualization motivate you to keep pushing forward?

As you step into this new chapter of your life, carry with you the wisdom, strategies, and inspiration you've gained. Embrace your role as an entrepreneur, a changemaker, and the architect of your destiny. The future is not something that happens to you; it is something you create with intention, passion, and relentless determination.

Thank you for allowing me to be part of your extraordinary journey. Here's to your boundless success and the incredible legacy you will forge. Go forth and change the world—one moneymaker at a time.

NOTES

NOTES

NOTES

NOTES

About the Author

Joses Ngugi is a Physical Therapist, dynamic public speaker, and co-founder of both Cash In Class University and Pre-PT Grind. With over seven years of experience, Joses has been instrumental in unlocking the potential of students and new graduates alike. His journey from a struggling student to a thriving entrepreneur and business coach showcases his dedication to helping others achieve financial freedom.

Joses, along with his business partner Dr. Casey Coleman, has guided thousands of Pre-PT students to secure spots in Doctor of Physical Therapy programs across the USA and Canada. Their innovative strategies have also enabled students, new grads, and young adults to earn between $2,000 and $30,000+ per month, with some of their clients still being in school. This empowerment has allowed many to graduate debt-free and start their careers with financial stability.

In addition to his work with young adults, Joses has successfully built multiple businesses generating over seven figures. His expertise in leveraging online platforms and entrepreneurial avenues has made him a sought-after speaker and coach. His passion for helping others discover and monetize their unique skills is evident in his book, "Unlock Your Hidden Income," which provides a step-by-step guide for young adults to achieve financial freedom.

Joses's dedication to his craft and his unwavering commitment to his clients and students have made him a respected figure in the field of personal and professional development. Through his work, he continues to inspire and empower individuals to break free from financial constraints and create lives of abundance and fulfillment.

YOUR FREE VIP TICKET

I am passionate about helping you unlock you hidden income and achieve financial freedom. To build on everything you've learned in this book, I've created a special one-hour training session just for you.

In this exclusive training, I'll share the exact steps I used to transform my skills and passio into a successful moneymaker. If you've enjoyed the insights in this book, you'll find th training invaluable.

We'll go deep into practical advice, real-life examples, and actionable steps to help you apply these strategies in your own life.

Visit UnlockYourHiddenIncome.com/training to access your free VIP training.

This training won't be available forever, as I regularly update my content to keep it fresh. Mak sure to take advantage of this opportunity while i still available.

UnlockYourHiddenIncome.com/training

Take Your Next Step with Us

Level 1: Speak with Our Team for Personalized Support

Hey there! You've made it this far, and I'm excited to see where your journey takes you next. If you're feeling like you could use a bit more personalized support to implement the strategies we've talked about, my team and I are here to help.

Just head over to **UnlockYourHiddenIncome.com/Call**, fill out a brief application, and book a time that works for you.

We'll chat about where you are, where you're feeling stuck, and how we can assist you. Think of this as your opportunity to get tailored advice and clear direction. No pressure, just a chance to see if working with us can help you make a bigger impact and generate more income.

Level 2: Join Our Impact to Income University Coaching Program

Ready to really dive in and get hands-on guidance? Our Impact to Income University coaching program might be the perfect fit. This is where many of our successful clients started. We offer a comprehensive year-long package that includes everything you need: guidance, tools, community, and accountability. Imagine having a team that's dedicated to helping you build your moneymaker, step by step. Interested?

Visit UnlockYourHiddenIncome.com/ImpactToIncomeProgram to see if you qualify. We can't wait to potentially work with you and help you achieve remarkable success.

Level 3: Apply for Our Six-Figure Mastermind

Already have a successful moneymaker and looking to scale up? Our Six-Figure Mastermind is designed for those who are ready to reach six and multiple six-figure incomes. This program focuses on leveraging technology, strategies, and expert guidance to elevate your business. If you're serious about maximizing your impact and income, this is the next step.

Head over to UnlockYourHiddenIncome.com/SixFigureMastermind to apply and see if you qualify. Let's work together to take your success to the next level.

References

1. The Institute for College Access & Success (TICAS). (2021). Student Debt and the Class of 2020. Retrieved from https://ticas.org/wp-content/uploads/2021/11/classof2020.pdf.
2. American Physical Therapy Association. (2021). Student Debt Survey. Retrieved from https://www.apta.org.
3. Bureau of Labor Statistics. (2020). Occupational Outlook Handbook: Physical Therapists. Retrieved from https://www.bls.gov/ooh/healthcare/physical-therapists.htm.
4. Gatto, J.T. (2002). The Underground History of American Education. Retrieved from https://archive.org/details/TheUndergroundHistoryOfAmericanEducationByJohn-TaylorGatto.
5. Bureau of Labor Statistics. (2023). CPI Inflation Calculator. Retrieved from https://www.bls.gov/data/inflation_calculator.htm.
6. McKinsey Global Institute. (2018). Notes from the AI frontier: Modeling the impact of AI on the world economy. Retrieved from https://www.mckinsey.com/featured-insights/artificial-intelligence/notes-from-the-ai-frontier-modeling-the-impact-of-ai-on-the-world-economy.
7. National Institutes of Health. (2020). Artificial Intelligence in Health Care. Retrieved from https://www.ncbi.nlm.nih.gov/pmc/articles/PMC7366949/.

8. World Economic Forum. (2020). The Future of Jobs Report 2020. Retrieved from https://www.weforum.org/reports/the-future-of-jobs-report-2020.

9. PwC. (2018). Sizing the prize: What's the real value of AI for your business and how can you capitalize? Retrieved from https://www.pwc.com/gx/en/issues/data-and-analytics/publications/artificial-intelligence-study.html.

10. MIT Technology Review. (2019). The global AI agenda. Retrieved from https://www.technologyreview.com/2019/11/21/131303/the-global-ai-agenda/.

11. Harvard Business Review. (2018). How AI Will Redefine Work. Retrieved from https://hbr.org/2018/01/how-ai-will-redefine-work.

12. FINRA Investor Education Foundation. (2018). National Financial Capability Study. Retrieved from https://www.usfinancialcapability.org/.

13. Georgetown University Center on Education and the Workforce. (2019). The College Payoff: Education, Occupations, Lifetime Earnings. Retrieved from https://cew.georgetown.edu/cew-reports/the-college-payoff/.

14. Federal Reserve Bank of New York. (2021). Quarterly Report on Household Debt and Credit. Retrieved from https://www.newyorkfed.org/microeconomics/hhdc.html.

www.ingramcontent.com/pod-product-compliance
Ingram Content Group UK Ltd.
Pitfield, Milton Keynes, MK11 3LW, UK
UKHW021838270726
14058UKWH00002B/218